Industrial Mission
in a Changing World

Industrial Mission in a Changing World

Papers from the Jubilee Conference of the
Sheffield Industrial Mission

Edited by
John W. Rogerson

Sheffield
Academic Press

Published by Sheffield Academic Press Ltd
Mansion House
19 Kingfield Road
Sheffield S11 9AS
England

Printed on acid-free paper in Great Britain
by Bookcraft Ltd
Midsomer Norton, Bath

British Library Cataloguing in Publication Data

A catalogue record for this book is available
from the British Library

ISBN 1-85075-620-1
ISBN 1-85075-791-7 pbk

CONTENTS

LIST OF CONTRIBUTORS

MICHAEL ATKINSON ministers in High Wycombe. He joined Sheffield Industrial Mission in 1960, later working at the General Synod and in USPG. He represented the European Industrial Mission at the WCC's Advisory group on Urban Industrial Missian and contributed to, and saw through press, Leslie Hunter's biography.

TONY ATTWOOD, senior chaplain, Teesside Industrial Mission, coalfield chaplain, Industrial Mission in South Yorkshire 1986–95, campaigned for the government to review the 1992 coal closure plan and argued strongly for the churches' practical involvement in the regeneration of mining communities.

PAUL BAGSHAW worked as Employment Issues Worker with Industrial Mission in South Yorkshire between 1975 and 1979. He is now an Anglican priest in the diocese of Southwell. He is the author of *The Church beyond the Church*.

CAROLINE BARKER BENNETT, director of education for Manchester Diocese, was an industrial chaplain with Northumbria Industrial Mission 1977–90. Her article is drawn from her research with women about their experience as industrial workers on Tyneside from the early 1930s to the 1980s.

VERNON BROOKE has worked in Industrial Mission for 25 years. He has been industrial chaplain in the Chesterfield area since 1984, and is secretary of Industrial Mission in Derbyshire. His paper reflects his interest in theology and spirituality in relation to secular life.

PETER CHALLEN Sloan Fellow of the London Business School, Fellow of the RSA, was senior chaplain of South London Industrial Mission from 1967 to 1996. His 'theological auditing' discipline deals in depth with the interpretation and application of biblical themes to work.

PETER COPE has done Industrial Mission work in Leeds, London, Worcestershire and the Black Country. He is at present ecumenical town centre chaplain in Telford. His paper is an extract from the PhD thesis he completed in 1991 at Manchester University.

JAMES HALL is a Baptist minister who is now a full-time industrial chaplain with Glamorgan Industrial Mission in South Wales. His research degree (University of Wales, 1988) looked at British Industrial Mission in the light of Baptist approaches to mission and ministry.

SUE HAVENS is an Anglican priest who serves the Diocese of Liverpool as a member of the Industrial Mission Team, with special responsibility for Unemployment Issues. She is also a theologian who works particularly in the areas of training and Christian Adult Education.

RACHEL JENKINS is joint executive secretary at the William Temple Foundation. For the past eight years she has been exploring with lay people their profound understanding of links between faith and living. She continues to have faith in their ability to break new grounds. Her professional background is in teaching and organising adult education in England and Wales, Tanzania and South Africa.

DAVID MCLELLAN is Professor of Political Theology at the University of Kent. He is widely known for his research and writing on Karl Marx and Marxism, and has published extensively on the subject. His book *Unto Caesar* was published in 1993, and explores the political relevance of Christianity.

CHRIS PERCY is a member of the North Humberside Industrial Mission Team. His paper is based on a dissertation for the Hull MA (Theological understanding Industrial Society.).

ANNE PRIMAVESI is an author and researcher. Her first book *Our God Has No Favourites* written with Jennifer Henderson considers links between the eucharist and liberation theology. Her more recent book *From Apocalypse to Genesis* discusses the links between ecology, feminism and Christianity.

HILARY RUSSELL is a senior research fellow in the European Institute for Urban Affairs, Liverpool John Moores University, and development director for Merseyside Churches' Urban Institute. She is chair of Church Action on Poverty and author of *Poverty Close to Home: A Christian Understanding*.

PETER SEDGWICK is assistant secretary of the Board of Social Responsibility of the Church of England. Until 1994, he was adviser in industrial issues to the Archbishop of York, and lecturer in the Theological Understanding of Industrial society at Hull University. His most recent book, *The Enterprise Culture* was published in 1992.

PETER SELBY is the William Leech Professorial Fellow in Applied Christian Theology and from 1984–92 was Bishop of Kingston-upon-Thames. In 1987 he chaired the national working group of the Church of England's Industrial and Economic Affairs Committee, which produced the report *Industrial Mission—an Appraisal*. He is author of several books, of which the most recent *Be-longing* argues for a more visionary and inclusive church.

JOHN WEAVER was senior lecturer in Geology at Derby College of Higher Education (Derby University) from 1971–1978. After ten years as minister of a Baptist church, he is now tutor in Pastoral Theology at Regent's Park College, Oxford.

MIKE WEST has worked in Industrial Mission since 1967, first in Industrial Mission in Hertfordshire and Bedfordshire and latterly as senior chaplain in South Yorkshire. Throughout that time he has experimented with different models of 'Doing Theology'. He is the course tutor for the Industrial Mission Induction training course.

INTRODUCTION

John W. Rogerson

An academic biblical scholar is not the most obvious, and certainly not the best qualified, person to edit and introduce a volume of essays on industrial mission. By way of explanation it can be said, first, that links beween the Sheffield Industrial Mission and the University of Sheffield go back a long way. In 1949 the university was the venue for a consultation organized by Bishop Leslie Hunter on how men in training for the ministry might be equipped to serve in an industrial society.[1] Then, several years later, the Mission's first and most famous industrial chaplain, Ted Wickham, used his tenure of the Sir Henry Stephenson Fellowship in the university to do the research that led to his classic book *Church and People in an Industrial City*.[2]

The second link in the chain derives from the contacts that I had with the mission soon after my arrival in Sheffield in 1979, as the new Head of Department of Biblical Studies. These contacts reached their high point, so far as I was concerned, in May 1981 when Raymond Draper spent a day showing me round various British Steel works in Rotherham. This visit, and other meetings that I had with people associated with the industrial mission, coincided with a growing conviction on my part that academic biblical studies needed to pay more attention to today's world. Happily, this was a conviction also felt by several of my colleagues in the department, and as liberation and feminist issues became more prominent on the agenda of biblical studies, so some of the undergraduate courses, not to mention a number of doctoral theses, concerned themselves with 'The Bible in the Modern World', to name one such course. A further outcome was that links were developed with the Urban Theology Unit

1. See P. Bagshaw, *The Church Beyond the Church: Sheffield Industrial Mission 1944–1994* (Sheffield: Industrial Mission in South Yorkshire, 1994), p. 17.
2. E.R. Wickham, *Church and People in an Industrial City* (London: Lutterworth), 1957.

in Sheffield, and the department played the major role in arranging for the university to validate the Master of Ministry degree of the Urban Theology Unit.

In view of what has been written it was not surprising that today's senior chaplain, Mike West, should approach me in 1993 to ask if the Department of Biblical Studies could help with the arrangements for the Jubilee Conference of the Industrial Mission in September 1994. I was glad to be approached, and I am most grateful to my colleague Meg Davies for representing me on the organizing committee. She also looked after the university side of holding the conference at Sorby Hall.

Academic biblical scholars who are also broadly committed to the church have a number of things in common with industrial missioners, and I propose to discuss these before considering how biblical studies and industrial mission might help each other. First, biblical scholars who also have a church commitment are outsiders so far as the churches are concerned. If, to refer to Paul Bagshaw's essay, industrial missioners work with one foot outside the church, biblical scholars work almost with two feet outside the church, with the result that, like industrial missioners, they see things differently from those 'with both feet firmly planted inside'.[3] What then, do biblical scholars see?

Bearing in mind that they are dealing with a favoured minority who are not neccessarily the most intelligent people in society, but who have been fortunate enough to benefit from the education system so as to enter higher education, they see young and mature students developing intellectually and taking their place in a world in which the churches have no relevance. In some areas of the humanities and social sciences—subjects such as English literature, history, philosophy, sociology and politics come readily to mind—students are engaged in quests for meaning, and for a just and humane world; which is one reason why subjects such as English Literature retain their great popularity in spite of all government attempts in the past thirty years to persuade more students to study subjects in pure science and in technology.

This student quest for meaning is matched by the number of philosophers and political scientists who are trying, in secular terms, to redeem the world from the inhumanity and moral chaos that they perceive within it. Thus, to mention three writers in whom I have a particular interest, Charles Taylor's *Sources of the Self* is full of theological langu-

---

3.   P. Bagshaw, 'Sheffield Industrial Mission: The Politics of Holiness', p. 21 below.

age such as 'epiphany', 'natural piety', 'manifestation which brings us into the presence of something which is otherwise inaccessible', 'a transformation of our stance towards the world whereby our vision of it is changed', 'the notion of grace'.[4] Jürgen Habermas works with a counterfactual view of what it means to be a human being, in order to analyse why it is that, in practice, humans fail so signally to be what they are.[5] There is thus a strong 'salvific' element in his work. Seyla Benhabib adds a feminist dimension to Habermas's work, seeking to overcome the divisions of a fractured world.[6]

To be a biblical scholar with a church commitment, and faced by what I have described, is to face both despair and hope: despair that the church appears to make no contribution to those wider searches for meaning; and hope that biblical scholars, if they can engage in dialogue with these currents of thought, will be pushing at open doors.

This leads to a second area of possible common interest between biblical scholars and industrial missioners which can be introduced by a passage in Paul Bagshaw's essay. Paul writes, in connection with attempts to realize faith 'beyond the walls of the church' and the conflict that this brings with the church as the sponsoring body of industrial mission:

> To realise faith in the secular world implies a desire to change that world. To attempt to act on that desire is to step into the political realm. This in turn implies an openness to the world, the possiblilty of the subversion of faith, and the probability of re-evaluation of the assumptions that originally motivated the mission. In turn this implies a potential critique of the sponsoring church, and of its conventional articulation of faith. This critique will be based and phrased in part in the language and categories of the world outside the church.[7]

This quotation is appropriate to biblical scholarship in several ways. Most obviously, it touches upon biblical criticism which, by studying the Bible 'like any other book'[8] inevitably questions procedures and results that

4.   C. Taylor, *Sources of the Self: The Making of the Modern Identity* (Cambridge: Cambridge University Press, 1989), pp. 383, 419, 449.

5.   Habermas has worked out his position in many publications over the past thirty years. For a useful introduction to his far from easy work see S.K. White, *The Recent Work of Jürgen Habermas: Reason, Justice and Modernity* (Cambridge: Cambridge University Press, 1988).

6.   S. Benhabib, *Situating the Self: Gender, Community and Postmodernism in Contemporary Ethics* (Cambridge: Polity Press, 1992).

7.   P. Bagshaw, 'The Politics of Holiness', p. 29 below.

8.   The phrase 'like any other book' was a slogan in the debates about biblical

have been hallowed for generations in the churches. This is why biblical criticism is still a stumbling-block to many church-goers. Yet the alternative is to put the Bible above criticism, which means denying that it belongs to the real world of the experience of ordinary church-goers. Again, if biblical scholars respond to the kind of issues raised by writers such as Charles Taylor and Habermas, biblical studies will take on a very different complexion from its (mistaken) image as 'Bible Studies' underpinning traditional church teaching, not to mention its traditional image as a value-free and purely historical discipline. Yet the alternative is to deny that biblical studies has anything to do with a world in which secular writers are asking fundamental questions about the nature of humanity and of justice.

Thus, industrial missioners and biblical scholars with a church commitment share the frustration of being committed to an institution (the church) which they can only serve in all honesty by taking up positions that are inevitably critical of it, and which lead to their being increasingly marginalized by the church. Yet they also meet each other head on at this point; for their principal concern is with the world and its problems and not with the church as an institution. It is on the basis of this mutual concern for the world, and for the questions that it raises about justice and what it means to be human, that industrial missioners and biblical scholars can help each other. How can this be done?

From the side of industrial mission the answer is given in the essays in the present volume; and not only biblical scholars will benefit from reading them. All readers will be confronted by a rich diversity of material which ranges from the history and theology of industrial mission, through prospects for its future in a world (in Britain) in which there is no longer any mass-employment heavy industry but rather an enterprise and management culture which could be liberating but is more likely to be oppressive, to matters such as theological audit of industrial processes, the empowering of women trades unionists in traditional male strongholds, and spirituality in a secular society. In short, these essays will enable readers to reflect upon the world of daily experience in a more informed and sensitive way.

From the side of biblical studies, the most obvious encouragement that can be given is an assurance that the use of the Bible in small or 'basic' study groups to try to make sense of issues such as poverty and

criticism in the nineteenth century. See my *Old Testament Criticism in the Nineteenth Century: England and Germany* (London: SPCK, 1984), p. 217.

justice is not an illegitimate practice and one to be frowned upon. Biblical studies has become much more pluralist in the past twenty years, and while its philological, historical and literary disciplines remain the indispensable foundation for any responsible interpretation of the Bible, they are now supplemented and enriched by approaches that are sensitive to issues of oppression, freedom, justice and the responsible use of the world's resources.

But there is another contribution to be made from the side of biblical studies, which can best be stated as a response to the following interesting paragraph from Paul Bagshaw's essay:

> Wickham had no qualms that industry, though far from perfect, was part of God's Providence. However, his stress on the direct relationship between God and industry marginalised the Church of England. Bishop Taylor put the Church first. The task of mission as he construed it was to bring people out of the world to personal salvation and into membership of the existing Church structures... Industry was theologically and morally a neutral setting in which chaplains might support Christian workers, offer pastoral care, and proclaim the Gospel.[9]

As a biblical (Old Testament) scholar writing in the mid-1990s, it seems to me that Wickham and Taylor, as reported by Paul Bagshaw, were both wrong. In my view, Wickham underestimated the ambiguous nature of everyday reality, including industry, and the impossibility of seeing within it any divine purpose or pattern that might make sense of the whole. To put it another way, it is as easy to see a malevolent providence at work in something such as heavy industry—for example, in accidents, industrial illnesses, inhumane conditions, unfair rewards, industrial disputes—as a beneficial providence. If one is going to make sense of industry in terms of a larger vision then one needs the resources of a believing community which is sustained in faith and hope by its heritage and its worship. In other words, one needs the church in some form or other if one is trying to make sense of the world from a Christian perspective.

Taylor's mistake, in my view, was also to underestimate the ambiguous nature of reality, including industry. Industry is not a neutral setting where chaplains can simply find opportunities for pastoral work. Industry, together with many other forms of employment (including that in universities) can be alienating, de-humanizing and oppressive. A theology which claims that God is the ultimate beginning and end of creation

9. P. Bagshaw, 'The Politics of Holiness', p. 23 below.

and which yet has nothing to say about oppressive structures in which humans may have to work in order to live, is at best inadequate and at worst, contradictory. In making these remarks, I must stress that I am responding to Paul Bagshaw's summary of the position taken by Wickham and Taylor rather than taking issue with their actual writings, although I have no reason to suppose that Paul has in any way distorted their views.

It is at this point that the Bible, and especially the Old Testament, has something to contribute to the discussion. The Old Testament emerged from a world less complex than our own, but one no less violent or ambiguous. War, famine, exile, displacement, poverty and injustice appear frequently in its pages. Further, to judge from some of the psalms of lament, the book of Job and Ecclesiastes, it was no easier then than it is now to see any principle of divine justice at work or any divine plan being realised in the events of daily life. Yet somehow, believers held on to the hope that the goodness and justice of God, for which they earnestly longed, would ultimately triumph; and they composed narratives that retold their own story in the light of that hope, and psalms that celebrated by way of anticipation the dawning of a new age. Further, their hope sustained them in their attacks upon the injustices of the powerful and upon corrupt popular and official religion, and it led them to make personal sacrifices on behalf of others. Their commitment to their vision remains a source of hope for believers today who share the same longings for the ultimate triumph of the goodness and justice of God.

What does this imply for the relation between church and society? It implies a servant church; a church that is not an end in itself, but whose function is to keep alive a vision that will sustain those who long and act to see God's goodness and justice established in the world. It implies a church that will be critical of the world and of itself in God's name; a church which, in its own structures and practices will seek to be an embodiment of God's goodness and justice. This is a long way from the original aim of industrial mission, which was to devise a way of getting working people into membership of the church; but it is, in my view, a biblical view of the church in relation to society, and one which has much to offer to industrial mission.

The papers that follow in this volume have been grouped by theme, beginning with those that deal with the history and theology of the industrial mission. Then follow contributions which discuss the current world in which industrial mission operates, and the collection concludes with essays that tackle specific issues. I have integrated the key-note lectures into this scheme rather than having them together at the beginning of the volume. The Jubilee Conference was an inspiring occasion, and I very much hope that the collected papers will be of great value to all who share the aims of industrial mission.

Sheffield Industrial Mission: The Politics of Holiness*

Paul Bagshaw

For 50 years Sheffield Industrial Mission (SIM) has exercised faithful discipleship in the factories and offices of South Yorkshire's industry and commerce.[1] Through this history I wish to explore a question that seems to me to be basic to mission:

> Faith may, at least in part, be construed as the assumption of a privileged relationship with God. In what ways might such faith be properly understood, expressed and realized in a world that already has a direct and continuing relationship with God?

It is, therefore, an exploration of issues around an approach to mission which is not founded on a contradistinction, overt or implicit, between Christianity and the world.

A Cook's Tour of Sheffield Industrial Mission

In 1944, as the tide of war was turning, Bishop Leslie Hunter invited 'Ted' Wickham to Sheffield and appointed him 'industrial padre'. There was no blueprint, and Wickham made what he could of the opportunities available to him in Sheffield's vast steel works that physically and economically dominated the city.

Hunter had initially conceived the Mission as one strand of a larger

---

*   This paper is based on P. Bagshaw, *The Church beyond the Church—Sheffield Industrial Mission 1944–1994* (Sheffield: IMSY, 1994). In the paper, 'Church' generally refers to the Church of England. Until 1983 Sheffield Industrial Mission was an Anglican enterprise with assistance from other denominations. When used more generically, especially in the latter sections of the paper, 'churches' refers to the organized structures and governance of church bodies. 'Politics' refers to the structured exercise of power in the public domain.

1.   In 1990 Sheffield Industrial Mission became Industrial Mission in South Yorkshire (IMSY). The earlier name is retained as historically more appropriate, and because the organization remains much more widely known by that name.

strategy. It was intended to help reforge a broken relationship between the Church and the industrial masses, and in doing so to counter society's growing amoral secularism. As Industrial Mission grew stronger it articulated its own goals, independent of Hunter's strategy. Wickham wanted to see God's will worked out in and through industry. Industry determined the shape of society; therefore embedding Christianity within industry would lead to the re-christianization of society.

Classical theory of foreign missions provided Wickham with the framework for his venture into the new mission fields of industry.[2] His first task was to live with the industrial working class and to imbibe its culture and language in order to translate the gospel into their vernacular. The goal—a 'new expression of the Church'—was a community of Christians with indigenous (that is, working class) leadership. In time this community would become a new, autonomous and full member of the Christian family. Wickham's official line was that industrial mission was complementary to the parochial structures. In reality he doubted that the Church of England could ever be reformed, and he did not keep this opinion private.

Wickham's method became known as the 'Sheffield model' of works visiting. He would obtain access to a works with the agreement of both sides of industry. Shop-floor visits were systematic and regular. He would convene informal 'snap-break' (meal-break) meetings. All of which enabled him to identify leaders who could create and sustain progressively more autonomous Christian discussion groups and worshipping groups, which would constitute the 'new expression of the church'.

In 1959 Wickham was made Suffragan Bishop of Middleton. In 1962 Leslie Hunter retired. They were replaced by people with very different views. Wickham was followed by Michael Jackson who wanted to move away from his predecessor's model, and perhaps also from under his shadow. John Taylor, a conservative evangelical, succeeded Hunter as Bishop. The consequent clash of personalities and theology dominated SIM in the mid-1960s.

The conflict focused on the sacking of two chaplains. It was also about the relationship of the Mission to the Church, and the nature of

---

2. In France Abbé Godin and others had already taken the conceptual step to perceiving sociologically defined segments of society as devoid of the gospel in nominally Christian countries. See H. Godin and Y. Daniel, *France: Pays de Mission*, published in English in *France Pagan? The Mission of Abbé Godin* (London: Sheed & Ward, 1949).

that Church. For Bishop Taylor the Church, as it was, was of God: sufficient, authoritative and determinative. It was intolerable that its agency
should assert, as Wickham had, that God was calling people not to enter
the Church of England. The conflict erased Wickham's approach, and
almost destroyed the organization.

To help reconstruct the Mission Bishop Taylor asked an industrialist,
'Tim' Forder, to report on its future. Forder began by reformulating
SIM's goals. They were drafted to contrast with what were perceived to
have been the ecclesiological and political errors of the 1950s. The
Mission's new task was to bring individuals into personal Christian
discipleship made visible in worshipping membership of a parish church.

In the first years following the conflict the Mission was highly sensitive to ecclesiastical suspicion. It courted acceptability in part by making
itself very 'churchy'. The Mission described industry as its parish, and its
staff as parish priests. Chaplains focused their activities firmly on the
individual. They supported Christians in industry, offered pastoral care,
and sought to evoke a personal faith.

By the end of the 1970s the Mission could relax, having re-established
ecclesiastical and ecumenical credibility. It began again to look beyond
the individual and to address the culture of industry. It also sought to
educate the Church on industrial matters, in the implicit conviction that
lack of understanding (rather than motivation) inhibited the Church's
ability to effect God's will in society.

In the 1980s the theme of 'justice' became central to the Mission.
Justice was understood as liberty and equality for all by virtue of their
status as children of God.[3] Progress towards justice was expressed in
the amelioration of, or opposition to, some of the goals, processes and
consequences of political and industrial culture.

The Mission and the Church

Apart from the isolation that followed the crisis of the mid-1960s, SIM
was an Anglican venture with assistance from other denominations. In
1983, after several years of discussion, it became a Local Ecumenical
Project (LEP) with a Council drawn from seven denominations as well
as from industry.

---

3.   There is an implicit paradox in appealing to God to legitimate action for
justice in the context of a (theoretically) democratic society, where legitimization is
grounded in the people.

The relationship between the Mission and the Church was the prime determinant of the self-understanding and parameters of industrial mission work. The Church of England, and latterly the denominations that contribute to the Mission's Council, sponsored, authorized and largely paid for the Mission. All mission, by virtue of being 'sent out', is inevitably located on the edge of a church, and thus invites suspicion and disregard. Yet unless this relationship is secure a mission has no more authority than a voluntary association.

One early tension lay in the question of whether any such mission was necessary. From the Church of England's perspective, Sheffield's industry was not a foreign mission field. Anglican parishes claimed a geographic hegemony over the cure of souls. Church structures had prior relationships with industry through lay Christians in the works and through links with industrial decision makers. Wickham's 'new expression of the Church' threatened this directly. A new church body would conflict with the existing pattern, however tenuous such contacts were in practice. The wider church never recognised the indigenous leadership Wickham built up in industry.

The Mission was the Church's agent in industry. Yet it was also partly founded on a critique of the Church and its role in the world, and it has almost always wanted the Church to be something different. The failure of the Church to accept its responsibilities in and to the secular world, or to respond adequately to the urgency and scale of the missionary challenge, was daily obvious to chaplains. Those working with one foot outside the Church will never see things from quite the same perspective as those with both feet firmly planted inside. The critique of the Church was based in part on this external perspective.

Furthermore, as perhaps for all Protestants, the Mission also drew authority directly from its relationship with God. In the 1950s and 1980s the mission at times espoused a 'prophetic' role in relation both to industry and to the Church. To be prophetic is to claim a more immediate relationship with God than that of the audience. It also asserts the Mission's authority over against that of the Church. This immediately raises the issue of conflicting authorities: whose privileged relationship with God should be heard over others?

In practice actual and potential tensions are reflected in, and contained by, the organizational structures of the Mission and its formal accountability to the Church. The conflict of the mid-1960s was as much a failure of organization as of theology. Administrative arrangements are attempts to embody faith and the mechanisms by which discipleship may be expressed in practical action. They also symbolize an organization's goals. Bishop Hunter regarded his advisory committee as a visible sign of industrial reconciliation. To the best of his knowledge it was the one Sheffield body on which managers and trades unionists sat down together on the same side of the table. The present LEP reflects a belief in the ecumenical integrity of the Mission and a desire to counter the scandal of denominational division. Perhaps church bodies in general may be described as attempts to realize transcendence through the coarse-grained medium of the committee.

The Mission and Industry

The Mission is largely autonomous in relation to industry, and largely subordinate to the Church, which curiously means it has greater potential to influence the Church than to influence industry. But the Mission is charged to work in industry. It has a representative and advocacy role on behalf of the Church, and of God, in a world where both Church and God may be deemed irrelevant. It is in secular industry that the Mission seeks to discover God and to realize discipleship. For most of its history the Mission has worked with individuals and, beyond them, addressed what it perceived to be the very heart of secular society.

British society primarily distributes income through employment, thus revealing how people are valued.[4] Industrial conflict, changes in the patterns of employment, and the changing relationship between those in work and those without it, all reflect and encapsulate broader relationships in society. Political conflict reveals both the distribution of power, and also the nature of conflicting aspirations for society. Political, moral and spiritual questions may be perceived with greatest acuity where these abstract relationships directly impinge on people's lives. God may be apprehended in the sufferings of others. Christian judgments on the ordering of society are honed in response to particular circumstances.

Indeed, discipleship is realized and God is made visible in the particularity of the Mission's actions. The foundation of the Mission's work has consistently been regular, sustained, undramatic works visiting. All other developments: pastoral care, discussion groups, links with trades unions and professional associations, training, worship and various projects were built on this foundation.

4.   Wealth is primarily distributed through inheritance.

Wickham had no qualms that industry, though far from perfect, was part of God's Providence. However, his stress on the direct relationship between God and industry marginalised the Church of England. Bishop Taylor put the Church first. The task of mission as he construed it was to bring people out of the world to personal salvation and into member- ship of the existing Church structures. While in theory industry might be judged by Christian beliefs and standards, in practice it was to be left to its own devices. Industry was theologically and morally a neutral setting in which chaplains might support Christian workers, offer pastoral care, and proclaim the Gospel.

Works visiting and projects in the 1980s were designed to address the 'determining realities' of society.[5] These were located in the nexus of economics and politics. Industry itself was viewed with ambivalence: its actions reflected and furthered injustice, and yet it was also capable of expressing God's justice, and God could act within it. Because of the sharp impact of political and social issues on people's lives, the shop- floor was the place where these themes might be explored with greatest clarity. Works visiting was the Mission's major source of information about society; and that in turn was the basis of its influence in the Church. Information was one means to the goal of greater justice in society, which goal inevitably brought chaplains into the political realm.

The Mission and Politics

I wish to distinguish two levels of analysis. The first is a diffuse level of broad political orientation. At this level the Church may be said to have a general affinity with certain trends or groupings in national politics without implying any formal relationship.[6] Such an affinity is often made explicit only when its unwritten assumptions have been transgressed.

In these broad terms the mission's political orientation has been left- of-centre. In the 1950s the tenor was that of corporatist trades unionism; in the 1970s it was liberal pluralist; and in the 1980s local socialist. These are vague generalisations. At no time would every member of the team have personally subscribed to the same political dogma.

The mission was also born with the ethos of post-war consensus poli- tics engraved onto its genetic code. It has, for example, consistently

5. I believe the phrase was first used in this context by Dr John Atherton.
6. This is separate from the Establishment of the Church of England, and its concomitant participation in the political structures.

supported moves towards industrial democracy. When the assumptions of consensus were discarded at the level of national politics, the Mission actively supported local consensual moves for the regeneration of the City of Sheffield. If being left-of-centre was not always in accord with the more general affinities of the Church, the stress on consensus almost certainly was.

The second level of analysis is involvement in particular public policies, whether in their formulation, or furtherance, or in opposition to them. Here lay much greater divergence of opinion about the proper role of the Mission.

Clerical political activism in the 1950s was nominally guarded by the doctrine of the 'autonomy of the secular'. This asserted that, under God, secular experts were the proper people to make secular decisions. Clergy might offer moral guidance, and individual pastoral support, but otherwise had no role in industrial or political decision taking. In practice, however, some Mission staff became actively involved in the local Labour Party, though in a personal rather than an official capacity.[7] Local politics was dominated by the Labour Party and trades unions. The Mission's extensive access to officials and workers at all levels, and their own considerable organization across the steel industry, gave them the potential (which they did not exercise) for significant local political influence.

Political pressure was also exercised in the opposite direction. In 1964–66 locally powerful trades unionists and industrial managers together lobbied Bishop Taylor either to come to a negotiated settlement, or to reinstate the sacked chaplains and to dismiss the senior chaplain instead. These arguments failed in part because Taylor saw the Church as separate from, indeed superior to, secular power structures. Consequently he remained immune to external pressures. The manner and the conclusions of the official Church enquiries into the dispute reinforced such ecclesiastical isolationism.

The Mission of the early 1970s, despite a plethora of industrial-political conflicts, largely avoided visible political action. In the second half of the decade the response to large scale unemployment—as a moral issue demanding practical action—managed to respect this stance, and simultaneously to involve well-informed campaigning and constructive practical work.

---

7. And also, it is alleged, in the Communist Party, though I have been unable to substantiate this.

The 1980s saw a sharper politicization of the Mission. It drank from more politically radical theological analyses, including Christian feminism and the Urban Rural Mission movement, the latter being informed by liberation theology. These offered discourses of politicized Christian faith, but perhaps the greater influence was the Mission's own involvement in politics. It joined high profile campaigns. Chaplains became active members of campaigning organizations. They participated in local partnerships of public and private sector bodies, and raised and debated political issues in church settings.

The Mission's politicization was possible only because the Church of England had shifted its stance towards political action. In 1979–80 the Mission was commended for its non-partisan ministry in the national steel strike. In 1992 it was commended for providing ammunition to Church leaders lobbying Conservative Members of Parliament to vote against their own government. During the 1980s the Church had become increasingly willing to act as a pressure group, publicly standing against the government on specific policy items.

Political activism in turn raised questions of power and legitimate Christian action. As the 1980s wore on, the Mission's tone changed audibly. The goal of working for God's justice moved from a corollary of the Mission's work to be its central purpose. The Mission retained its generalized aspirations of seeking God's justice for all, and of embedding Christian values in society. Such goals, however, were increasingly expressed in smaller and more practical actions. Furthermore, in its 1990 Mission Statement, IMSY declared for the first time its opposition to destructive and oppressive practices alongside its hope for justice. In so doing it explicitly placed the struggle for justice above the desire for tolerance and unity in the canon of Christian virtues.

Political action requires both detailed information and an evaluative framework. The issue of the language, categories and concepts in which Christianity might be audible in a secular world was a key theological issue of the 1960s. Thereafter it became a practical issue: the choice to avoid theological jargon acknowledged the unfamiliarity of such terms outside Christian circles, but did not change the content of the message. The same attention, I suggest, has not been paid to the language and analytical disciplines appropriate to proper Christian political judgments and action, at least in Britain. Economics, sociology and political science, as well as theology, each appear inadequate to the task of relating simultaneously to God and to power.

Political commitment requires practical expression. The Mission remained dependent on industrial management and on the church hierarchy for its continued functioning. These relationships limited the degree of sophistication and precision with which the Mission could ask and answer questions of power, of proper social order, and of what exactly God's justice might constitute in practice. Its licence to engage in political action did not extend to the challenging of its masters.

The Church, the Mission, the World and God

The relationship of Sheffield Industrial Mission to both Church and industry may be described more as serial monogamy than as an unbroken marriage. It has, in effect, tried three or four different missions. Each has been characterized by a different theological perspective and has been undertaken in a changing social, political and industrial context. Each phase of the Mission's life has explored in different ways the nature of Christian discipleship in the industrial world.

Discipleship is in its essence paradoxical. It is participation in the transcendent, in God, in eternal life; yet it is only realized, understood and made visible in the material, secular, temporal world. It is the response of the created to the creator; yet creation simultaneously reveals and conceals God. God dwells in us, and we dwell in God, and yet we remain obdurately apart from God.

Churches dwell in God, and God in them. They comprise communities of the redeemed living out their faith in the world. They are charged with the responsibility of keeping faith with the inheritance of the Gospel and the Christian tradition as they received it, of preserving it and of handing it on to each successive generation. As human institutions churches operate in the temporal, secular world, and they do so in the ways of, and on the terms of, that world. A church is a holy people which participates in the transcendent—and a mundane corporation with interests to defend.

Industrial Mission (and perhaps any mission), though part of the Church, has a more particular commission: to be a medium by which Christian faith may be realised in the heart of secular society. Bishop Taylor apparently perceived the Mission as reaching out from the Church into a separate, godless world. This proved unsustainable as a basis for mission. More often, chaplains spoke of 'discovering' God in the world, and of recognizing the innate faith of many who had no contact with churches. They proceeded on the understanding that the Kingdom of God, at least in part, was to be realized in tangible freedoms and well-being in daily life. They proclaimed God's hope and saving purpose for humanity in terms of changing society.

The world, both physical creation and human society, has a much more diffuse relationship with God. God is creator, sustainer and redeemer. God also chose to enter the flux of the world through his incarnation in Jesus of Nazareth. All this simultaneously conveys both the intimacy and the otherness of God.

Church, mission and world each embody the paradox of discipleship, and each has its distinctive and restless covenant with God. The inter-relationship between these shared and divergent discipleships offers a dynamic framework within which faith is located and realized.

The Politics of Holiness

To reiterate the original question: Faith may, at least in part, be construed as the assumption of a privileged relationship with God. In what ways might such faith be properly understood, expressed and realized in a world that already has a direct and continuing relationship with God?

First, churches are primary. Without them the question cannot be asked. Without them there is no gospel, no Christianity and thus no Christian discipleship. A church has authority to determine what may or may not constitute legitimate Christian belief and action and it alone can legiti-mate or exclude forms of discipleship. Consequently all mission is dependent upon a church. Missions can only legitimately act in the world whilst they remain within whatever bounds are set by the sponsoring church.

The primacy of the church is not an abstract matter. Churches are latent battlefields: to control a church's committees and structures is to have both the authority and the power to advance one conception of Christianity, and to exclude others. As Elizabeth Schüssler Fiorenza writes:

> ...while some feminists relinquish religion as hopelessly patriarchal, the Right claims the power to name and to define the 'true' nature of biblical religions over against liberation theologies. These well-financed and well-organized reactionary religious groups are often linked with right-wing financial and political institutions. They collaborate in the religious defense of capitalist patriarchy by bad-mouthing emancipatory

movements and theologies in general and feminist theology and the feminist movement in particular, declaring them to be un-Christian and anti-church.[8]

To fail to engage with such forces leaves power unchallenged in reactionary hands.

No church is in fact wholly self-contained or self-sufficient, despite all efforts to make it so. Their role and responsibility as guardian of the faith, as well as organizational and psychological pressures, inevitably lead churches to demarcate themselves from the external wo.ld. One consequence is that churches tend to act as though God had no direct relationship with creation apart from the Church. Another is to gloss over political implications of salvation, and to disown politically active discipleship. In part this stems from a recognition that political engagement implies both a desire to change society, and a vulnerability to being changed by society. Ecclesiastical identity is partially constructed in opposition to the surrounding world, and thus to challenge this demarcation is to unsettle a church's identity. The potential threat to the identity and integrity of the Church from the intrusion of the external, transient, godless world would appear to be more powerful than the implications of faith for public political action.[9]

Theology is part of the assertion of separation. To the extent that theological discourse reflects and serves the contradistinction between church and world, so it is inadequate to describe or evaluate that world, and resistant to attempts to engage secular disciplines.

The experience of the Mission has been that its discipleship, its attempt to realize faith beyond the walls of the Church, cannot be done within this assumption of opposition. To realize faith in the secular world implies a desire to change that world. To attempt to act on that desire is

8.   E. Schüssler Fiorenza, *Discipleship of Equals: A Critical Feminist* Ekklesia-*logy of Liberation* (London: SCM Press, 1993), pp. 2-3

9.   A wide array of reasons have been adduced for this aspiration to autarchy and for non-participation, most of which may be reduced to the statement that Christians have no will to be involved. There is an important asymmetry here: it is easy to find sufficient reasons for inaction, and very hard to find a reason of sufficient strength to begin and sustain common political action.

An alternative approach has been to address the external world according to purely theological presuppositions, or undiluted biblical precepts. This can produce active Christian engagement with secular affairs at the cost of denigrating the world by contrast with God's Kingdom. The extent of (or even the concept of) theological or biblical 'purity' must also be subject to question.

to step into the political realm. This in turn implies an openness to the world, the possibility of the subversion of faith, and the probability of re-evaluation of the assumptions that originally motivated the Mission. In turn this implies a potential critique of the sponsoring church, and of its conventional articulation of faith. This critique will be based and phrased in part in the language and categories of the world outside that church. The seeds of conflict germinate when such thought is translated into action. Integral to the theological dispute, such conflict is likely to focus on what is authoritative and who can decide. It will therefore involve a tussle in, and for control of, precisely those organs of authority that will eventually determine the conflict. In the end, a prophetic claim to a superior privileged relationship with God cannot outweigh the authority of a church as guardian of the historic faith.

Churches and missions have a shared discipleship. Both are concerned with the discernment, the proclamation and the realization of God's purpose for the world: salvation. To be saved is to live in God, and yet, this side of death, such salvation can only be expressed within the complexities of the material, social world.

Churches and missions also have distinct roles. Missions cannot function without a church and no church can be whole without mission. The bureaucracy of both church and mission must be adequate to mediate the differences between them and to contain any potential conflict. To construct and maintain such structures requires considerable political skill.

Church, mission and world share a relationship with God, and each relationship is unique. To explore the interrelationship between them in such a manner as to evoke and explore discipleship in all its paradoxical fullness requires a discourse adequate to discuss God, creation and human power in the same sentence.

Talking of Politics and Transcendence

The purpose of such a discourse would be to enable, encourage and validate the expression and realisation of faith in the secular world. It would have the potential to enable missions to travel further from their sponsoring churches while retaining authorization and accountability. It would be grounded in theological categories because it is motivated by faith, and open to secular categories because it concerns the realization of faith. It would also be opposed by those whose conceptions of Christianity are grounded in the opposition between churches and the secular world, and for whom the purpose of mission is to extract people from that world. Born in conflict, it would be a discourse committed to a particular emancipatory conception of Christianity, and actively opposed to the forces of reaction.

One possible approach would be to begin with salvation. Salvation is both from the world, and for it; both apart from the world and in its midst. It is liberation from oppression and convention. It is experienced as a transformatory leap into eternal life and as unsteady progress towards God. It is expressed through the conversion of individuals, and through the progressive enhancement of personal and collective liberties, well-being (perhaps prosperity) and justice, irrespective of religious adherence. Physical creation itself can receive salvation, greater recognition of which may engender a more positive valuation of the material world, including human physicality, within Christian faith.[10]

The style of this discourse would be tentative, provisional and concerned with particularities. It would counter any attempt to construct and apply precast theological certitude. It would rather seek to discover and further God's kingdom within the complexities and ambiguities of the world. It would constantly struggle to hold together the paradoxical nature of salvation. Its central problem would be the discernment, in theory and in practice, of exactly how and where God may be glimpsed, and which particular human actions further God's purposes. It would be expressed in practical action to struggle against all forms of oppression, violence, insecurity and exploitation.

Such a discourse would have to be located in the lifeblood of the churches. To attempt an independent, external construction would be an exercise in theological Esperanto. The discernment of salvation and the validation of discipleship is an exercise of authority. It will be mediated through and embodied in a church's synods, conferences, boards and committees. Because it is an approach at some variance from many conceptions of Christianity its advocacy will be a matter of hard political struggle. The political prize is the ability to shape the nature of contemporary Christianity, and to set the faces of churches against the powers of this world.

For such a discourse to be heard implies a new sense of Christian identity. A church which shared this identity would celebrate the relationship God now enjoys with human society and physical creation, and be more open to God's world beyond its walls. It would become more cautious and less dogmatic and more assertive for justice. IMSY, other

10. Rom. 8.20-22; Col. 1.15-20.

industrial missions and many other bodies can contribute to this process. I believe that many churches have already travelled a long way along this route, although not in Britain. Others, however, will resist it with every prayer in their body. To grasp this nettle is a political task of holiness.

'I HAVE CALLED YOU FRIENDS'—MISSION AND MOTIVE

Michael Atkinson

1910, 1944, 1964, 1994

'The Evangelization of the World in this Generation', the slogan of the World Missionary Conference held in Edinburgh in 1910, had a short shelf-life. A mere four years later the 'Christian' West collapsed in a brutal civil war. The irony of this was entirely clear to Leslie Hunter, then thirty, but at fifty, as Bishop of Sheffield from 1939, he still found himself ill-prepared for ministry in a post-christendom age. His *Diocesan Newsletter* of November 1941 records the situation he found himself faced with— empty churches and an unresponsive Church.[1] Ted Wickham, Hunter's first industrial chaplain, observed that while in earlier centuries the churches had lost (or, failed to gain) the working classes, in our own century they had lost the middle classes too.[2]

Bishop Hunter recognized the cultural divide that separated many folk from the organized life of the churches. He realized that people who could not understand poetry would never find themselves at home in worship. Christians had become what the sociologists call a 'cognitive minority'. Twenty-five years after Hunter's 1941 reflections, Simon Phipps, later Bishop of Lincoln, found it useful to borrow an image from the Italian novelist Lampedusa to illustrate the strategic position of the churches. The King of Naples had been conscientious enough at his desk

---

1.   L.S. Hunter, *The Bishop's Letter* (Sheffield, 15 November 1941). See M.H. Atkinson, '"An Episcopal Fly on the Walls of British Industry"', in G. Hewitt (ed.), *Strategist for the Spirit: Leslie Hunter, Bishop of Sheffield 1939–62* (Oxford: Becket Publications, 1985), pp. 157ff.

2.   E.R. Wickham, *Church and People in an Industrial City* (London: Lutterworth Press, 1957). This work has been substantially criticised now by J. Morris, 'Church and People Thirty-Three Years On: A Historical Critique', in *Theology* 94.758 (London: SPCK, Mar.–Apr. 1991), pp. 92-101.

but all the while the course of history had been flowing 'in another valley'.[3]

Hunter and Wickham believed that the distance between the Church and the ordinary non-attender was not actually so great as to be unbridgeable. One leg of their twofold strategy is well remembered, but the other made little headway: to prepare the churches, by an internal reformation, for the arrival of new people, found through theologically defensible friendships pursued outside the churches. They maintained their strategy for nearly twenty years—as long as either of them was in Sheffield. Only after they had both left did argument about the lengths to which matters should go come into the open.

A simple anecdote from the 1960s illustrates the missionary situation at that time. An attempt was being made to attract new people to the monthly Eucharist of the Mission in Sheffield Cathedral, a service considerably simplified from what was then canonically permitted. Three or four office workers made the jump, but the shop-floor people all jibbed. The concessions the churches had made towards them had not been sufficient. Before he had come to Sheffield, Hunter had written that

> there will always be something singularly unconvincing in an institution preaching the Cross and pleading the Cross upon its altars, if it has little of the Cross in its common life and is always desperately afraid to die.[4]

Now we find an editorial during the James Bulger case wistfully remarking that the Church has 'allowed itself to lose its audience'.[5] If contact is to be re-established, what kind of death must the Church really endure? This is a question which foreign missionary societies have from their outset faced. They have massive experience upon which the rest of us could draw.

The Councils of the Churches

International church councils have been well ahead in new thinking. In 1963 the Commission on World Mission and Evangelism of the World Council of Churches (CWME), in a conscious new start in the process post 1910, summed up its position in the phrase 'mission in six

3. S.W. Phipps, *God on Monday* (London: Hodder & Stoughton, 1966), p. 11.
4. The Archdeacon of Northumberland (L.S. Hunter), 'The Church and the Ministry', in *International Review of Missions* (London: Oxford University Press, XXVI, 1937), pp. 230ff.
5. *The Independent*, 28 November 1993.

continents'.[6] In this it reflected what Hunter had been writing in Sheffield in 1941, and Godin and Daniel in France in 1943—namely, that our own continent, that of Edinburgh, Sheffield and Paris, was 'pays de mission' just like the others.[7]

Similar insights emerged at about the same time within the Roman Catholic world at the Second Vatican Council, to be kept alive in subsequent Apostolic Exhortations.

> Strata of humanity are transformed: it is a question not only of preaching the Gospel in ever-wider geographic areas or to ever greater numbers of people, but also of affecting and as it were challenging, through the power of the Gospel, mankind's criteria of judgment, determining values, points of interest, lines of thought, sources of inspiration and models of life.[8]

In purely Anglican circles, as long ago as 1973 the Anglican Consultative Council declared:

> The missionary task of the Church continues to be that of reconciling man to God, man to man, and man to his environment. The oneness of the missionary task throughout the world has been emphasized in recent years in all parts of the Christian Church. The emergence everywhere of autonomous churches in independent nations has challenged our inherited idea of mission as a movement from 'Christendom' in the West to the 'non-Christian' world. In its place has come the conviction that there is but one mission in all the world, and that this one mission is shared by the world-wide Christian community... The oneness of the missionary task must now make us all both givers and receivers.[9]

Light from the East

It is unlikely that the Western missionary societies of the Church of England would on their own have come to these conclusions. It was the younger churches that produced the stimulus for change. Here are some examples.

---

6.   R.K. Orchard (ed.), *Witness in Six Continents* (London: Edinburgh House Press, World Council of Churches, Division of World Mission and Evangelism, 1964), pp. 173-75.

7.   M. Ward, *France Pagan? The Mission of Abbé Godin* (London: Sheed & Ward, 1949).

8.   Paul VI, *Evangelii Nuntiandi* (Rome, 1975; ET: London: The Catholic Truth Society), p. 19.

9.   Anglican Consultative Council, *Partners in Mission* (London: SPCK, 1973), p. 47.

1. Ronald Hall, Bishop of Hong Kong (and ordainer of Florence Li), had been close to Hunter throughout the 1920s. He had gone on to encounter at first hand a missionary situation in China, for centuries impervious to Western Christian missions. Hall felt it important, not just missiologically but also theologically, to emphasize the human dimension in all church relationships. Thinking of Jesus washing his disciples' feet, he is moved by 'both holiness and the human joy of touching and tending the bodies of those we love'. For Hall, mission is an adventure in friendship, and from the shared basis of a common discipleship: 'The Adventurer in friendship takes life as it comes, the rough or the smooth will be all one to him (or to her) if it is *for* people and *with* people.'[10]

2. Philip Wickeri, also working in China, builds on Hall and emphasizes the artistic nature, rather than the strategic intent, of mission: 'Protestants...need to become more familiar with the creation-centred tradition associated with the Eastern Orthodox, the Catholic and the Anglican communions... developing an understanding of structure which embraces the sacramental nature of reality.'[11]

Friendship, for Wickeri, is an 'order of creation' alongside the more orthodox orders (or 'mandates' in Lutheran terminology) of marriage, government or Church. And Wickeri's treatment of mission as an *art* responds, he believes, to the way in which God's love contrives the creation and the sustenance of the world.

He quotes a Japanese Catholic novelist. The most important thing about Jesus's life was that he was never known to desert people in trouble:

When women were in tears, he stayed by their side. When old folks were lonely, he sat with them quietly. It was nothing miraculous, but the sunken eyes overflowed with love more profound than a miracle. And regarding those who deserted him, those who betrayed him, not a word of resentment came to his lips. No matter what happened, he was the man of sorrows, and he prayed for nothing but their salvation.[12]

10. R.O. Hall, *The Art of the Missionary* (London: SCM Press, 1942), pp. 40, 30.

11. P.L. Wickeri, 'Friends Along the Way', in *Theology*, 93.753 (London: SPCK, May–June, 1990), p. 189.

12. P.L. Wickeri, 'Friends', pp. 105-106, quoting S. Endo, *A Life of Jesus* (trans. R.A. Schuchert; Tokyo: Charles Tuttle, 1980), p. 85.

A rather Johannine view of the Christ, indeed, but one recalls that in the 1960s failed Sheffield experiment over the Eucharist one of the shop-floor workers left behind the comment that what he needed most from the Church was not its traditional symbols so much as companionship, the sense of 'not being alone'.

3.   Aloysius Pieris is a Sri Lankan Jesuit, a 'liberation theologian', from a culture unlike Latin America and closer to China in not having been heavily penetrated by Christianity. He finds Asian society interestingly parallel to our Western, post-christendom, commercial and 'development' culture, and identifies the current missionary crisis in Asia as one of authority—those who wield authority see the crisis as one of obedience: to the rest it is 'a crisis of credibility'.[13] That is probably quite close to what produced the problems in Sheffield in the mid-1960s. Pieris stands with colleagues in the Ecumenical Association of Third World Theologians in looking for authentication in mission to come from those who are missionized. In Asia this means almost exclusively the poor. Church life in Asia thus provides models of operating outside historic 'christendom' and within cultures as full of other competing religions and ideologies, as of course is ours in the West. Pieris believes: 'Inasmuch as all these religions and ideologies claim to be liberative movements, saviours of the masses, *it is only the poor who decide who is competent to liberate them.*'[14]

This should not sound strange to Western ears. Charles Booth in 1903 observed,

> The British working man, if he awakes at all from indifference is hostile... His active interests are much more commonly political than religious... The mass of the people make no profession of faith and take no interest in religious observances...[They] remain alienated or unconcerned.[15]

Robert McCall, the founder of the *Mission Populaire Evangélique de France* as long ago as 1871, told a similar tale. He was distributing

---

13. A. Pieris S.J., *An Asian Theology of Liberation* (Edinburgh: T. & T. Clark, 1988), p. 35.

14. A. Pieris, *Theology*, pp. 36-37. Pieris's emphasis.

15. C. Booth, *Life and Labour of the People of London—Third Series: Religious Influences* (London: Macmillan, 1902), p. 258.

evangelical tracts when a man without much English but with quite
sufficient intelligence told him: 'Thanks, we'll not have religion just
pushed at us, but if one of you's got the sort of religion that'll really
liberate us from our situation, a lot of us'll come along.'[16]

Pieris's observations could be valuable to churches beyond his own.
At Lambeth Conferences older African bishops warn newer ones, scan-
dalized by the de-christianization of 'Christian' England, against being
unsympathetic and censorious. England today prefigures their own
coming cultural setting. Compare, Hunter, Godin, CWME, Vatican II
and ACC. Truly there is but one world, and one mission.

4.   A final witness from Asia is another Sri Lankan Jesuit, Michael
     Amaladoss, highly regarded among Catholic missionaries. He
     believes that, even post-Vatican II, Catholic missions remain
     'top-down' and centralist. Being himself on the periphery and
     'from below', Amaladoss warns against mission-as-inculturation-
     as-domestication. Instead, mission must be prophetic, and that
     can be counter-cultural. He quotes CWME with approval:
     'Proclamation is always linked to a specific situation and a
     specific moment in history. It is God's good news contrasted
     with the bad news of that specific situation.'[17]

'The Gospel is good news, not bad olds!', as Walter Hollenweger, one
time Professor of Mission in the Selly Oak Colleges in Birmingham, used
to put it. It is always a call to conversion, and to Pieris that means *from*
inequality, consumerism and violence, both communally and interna-
tionally. Judged in those terms, 'not only primary evangelization, but the
ongoing challenge of the Gospel is needed everywhere', particularly in
the 'first world', where in a post-christendom age sensitivity to the
challenge of the gospel has become blunted:

> I wonder whether, in a world that is becoming increasingly a global
> village, a re-evangelization of the Christian world may not be a more
> credible witness today to the rest of the world. Such an effort would also

16. J.-P. Morley, *1871–1984—La Mission Populaire Evangélique—Les
Surprises d'un Engagement* (Paris: Les Bergers et les Mages, 1993), p. 19. (My
translation.)

17. M. Amaladoss S.J., 'Misssion: From Vatican II into the Coming Decade', in
International Review of Mission, 79.314 (Geneva: World Council of Churches,
Commission on World Mission and Evangelism, Report of the Melbourne confer-
ence of te Commission, 1980), p. 195.

lead us to re-examine the cultural and historical structures in which we carry the challenge of the gospel in our mission *ad extra*, especially if they have not had much success at home...

The church today is called to commit itself to an international moral movement of peoples. It is in pilgrimage towards the reign of God in the company of all people of good will. It has to be true to its own identity as the witness of the good news of Jesus, of his death on the Cross and of his resurrection. It has also to hear the call to be the servant of unity in the world. While being a community rooted in Jesus, it needs to have open frontiers, ready to dialogue with everyone. Opting for the poor, it must prophetically confront the unjust oppressor. In humility, it has to be sensitive to the mystery of the action of God in the world. It should be open to the creative newness of the Spirit. Its horizon is God's own mission of universal reconciliation, when God will be with God's people.[18]

An end to mission-as-domestication: 'mission without mystery is oppressive.'[19]

Barely hidden beneath all these reflections coming from Asia is the charge that Western churches have not always behaved in a spirit of humility before God, and they have not always conducted their missions in a spirit of friendship. Mission has too often been oppressive. It has come from churches which assume that, like the sons of Zebedee, they have a claim to be enthroned in some 'right-hand' place in the scheme of salvation. Their 'good news' is for others, not themselves. For them, in fact, it is 'old'—a known product simply requiring marketing. How different from the Asian in the story who likens mission to 'one beggar telling another where bread is to be found'. A mission more marked by friendship would be far more egalitarian.

Western Agreement

Happily, such insights are not now so strange in the West. Theologians and ethicists here are beginning to recognize the flawed nature of some of our inherited models of mission, and indeed of God. Grace Jantzen uses theories of the development of human personhood to underpin an appeal for connectedness and solidarity, urgently needed before we destroy the biosphere lent to us by God.[20] The levelling ecological threat

18. M. Amaladoss, 'Mission', pp. 219-20.

19. M. Amaladoss, 'Mission', p. 212.

20. G. Jantzen, 'Connection or Competition: Identity and Personhood in Christian Ethics', in *Studies in Christian Ethics* 5.1 (Edinburgh: T. & T. Clark, 1992), pp. 1-20.

is also behind Sallie McFague's appeal for a recovery of models of God as lover and friend. The Enlightenment brought with it the paradigm shift that the world, even if it remains God's, is also very much ours, and we make and unmake it as also we make and unmake ourselves. If we do not 'accept responsibility for our beautiful, fragile earth...there will be no bread and no wine'.[21] It is as lover, rather than Lord, that God is most credible as a saviour amid present dangers. As friend, rather than judge, God is companion and sustainer.

Conclusion

Nearly thirty years after leaving Sheffield, I find myself engaged at both ends of the divide Hunter and Wickham sought to bridge. I read with affection and admiration of the work of full-time industrial mission, and of reflective agencies such as the William Temple Foundation.[22] But I am acutely aware of the vulnerability, financial and political, of all that. More theological allies would help. Whatever else we need, then, I believe that theological exploration is basic for the whole Christian experiment, for the sake of the world and the larger church just as much as for the survival of industrial mission.

With hindsight, some of the early belief and practice in Sheffield looks now like a not-fully-conscious stumbling towards these insights, coming in from our councils, foreign churches and academia. The questions these fellow-workers address, missiological and theological, are pertinent to British parish ministries as well as to other specialisms. Are we sufficiently aware of them?

In the early 1970s a North American 'Task Force' distinguished 'genitive' theology (which takes a topic and does theology 'about' it from some distance) from 'dative' theology (reflection by a group upon its own experience, then 'shared').[23] Better than either would be 'joint' reflection by people with wide varieties of experience and skill—'ablative' theology. David Jenkins, then at the William Temple Foundation, once

21. S. McFague, *Models of God: Theology for a Nuclear Age* (London: SCM Press, 1987), p. 187.

22. See most recently R.H. Preston, M. Brown, R. Jenkins and A. Addy, *Archbishop William Temple: Issues in Church and Society 50 Years On* (Manchester: William Temple Foundation, 1994).

23. D.E. Jenkins, 'Concerning Theological Reflection', in *Study Encounter* SE/11, 7.3 (Geneva: World Council of Churches, 1971).

called for this in a threefold schema for problem-solving contributed to by 'inhabitants', 'experts' and 'fixers', not usually the same people. In the complex new situations we all now live in this seems incontrovertible.

At an earlier stage Industrial Mission profited greatly from face-to-face encounters with theologians of world rank. I am not aware that those kinds of contact now exist. But how can the 'theological backbone'[24] which both Church and world need be grown other than by a coalition of people engaged in a mission at many different points in dialogue with, or at least reading of, missiologists and theologians of both East and West? Such dialogue, it could be argued, would be the only valid response, out of shared humility and vulnerability, to the one creating and sustaining God, who declares, after all, 'I have called you friends'.[25]

24. L.S. Hunter, *Bishop's Letter*.
25. Jn 15.15.

DOING THEOLOGY: A MODEL EXAMINED

Mike West

Introduction

This paper explores Industrial Mission in South Yorkshire's operational
need to have an Applied Theology, and how it has tried to create contextual theologies. It describes a model derived from the work of Ian
Fraser. It reports on the use of this model in the training of Industrial
Mission staff, and concludes that it is basically valid but requires further
more detailed study.

The Need for a Model

In 1944, the year that Bishop Leslie Hunter appointed Ted Wickham to
be the first industrial chaplain in Sheffield, he wrote in his Visitation
Charge 'that the church was trying to tackle the issue of an industrial
world with the tools of a pre-industrial one, though the two hardly
touched'.[1] Ever since, Industrial Missions have claimed that their task
included 'developing Christian traditions of thinking and practice through
the industrial realities they were involved in'.[2]

Ian Fraser stressed that this is an activity of the whole church:

> The Christian community, through their daily immersion, in life, are in
> contact with God's healing and upsetting presence. Their reflection on
> questions and insights produced by their attempts to be his people,
> wherever they are and whatever they do, is theology.[3]

---

1. *Thinking in Practice—Theology and Industrial Mission* by members of the
Industrial Mission Association Theology Development Group, IMA TDG 3 (1980),
p. 16.

2. *Thinking in Practice*, p. 1.

3. I.M. Fraser, *Re-Inherit the Church!* (World Council of Churches Study
Encounter, 7.4; Geneva: WCC, 1971), p. 3.

Industrial chaplains inhabit the boundary of industry and the church, often feeling that they do not belong to either. They have a pressing need to understand their own position and motives. They also need to be able to justify their activities and policies to industry and the Church using terms that can communicate in each setting.

> It [Industrial Mission] has been from the beginning an extended seminar in applied theology, conducted in an unfamiliar setting [the workplace] and with no guaranteed audience. In the process of clarifying its own mission it has raised issues about the mission of the whole Church in the world.[4]

The general assertion that new tools are needed does not create them. Connecting the 'tradition' and the 'industrial realities' always contains the strong possibility that one is being forced to fit into the mould of the other. Some have concentrated on discovering in the tradition aspects of Christian understanding relevant to the industrial situation. There are many rich seams to be mined, much of which is scarcely mentioned in traditional theological education.

But are these pre-industrial tools valid for the industrial age? Deductions from formulations which were developed by male church officials, sepa-rated from mainstream economic activities, in relatively rich Europe stand accused of being tainted with sexism, nationalism, racism and imperialism. Christian Schumacher, a white male, European professional has provided a good example of the strengths and limitation of a deductive model.[5]

A purely inductive approach can be similarly criticized for the dis-tortions arising from the standpoint and experience of the theologian. For example, Christine Schaumberger criticizes some feminist theologians because of their omission of women's experience of work.[6] Whatever its limitations, Industrial Mission has usually preferred to work with inductive or contextual models. It was the industrial context, including their own

---

4.   *Industrial Mission—An Appraisal* (the Report of a Working Party chaired by Bishop Peter Selby, for the Board for Social Responsibility of the Church of England; London: BSR, 1988), p. 49.

5.   C. Schumacher, *To Live and Work: A Theological Interpretation* (Bromley: Marc Europe, 1987).

6.   C. Schaumberger, 'Sharing and Feeding the Hunger for Bread and Roses; Towards a Critical-Feminist Theology of Women's Work', *Concilium* (1993), p. 118.

ambiguous position in it which was the driving force behind their attempts to (as they labelled it) 'Do Theology'.[7]

The Genesis of the Model

Industrial Mission found allies in the inductive approach in the World Council of Churches. The Laity department, in which Ian Fraser worked in the 1970s, focused on the Church in the World. The WCC Humanum Study, of which David Jenkins was the Director from 1969, began with the question 'how far and in what ways can men and women tolerate change?' This programme established a number of Task Forces to look at the role of Christians in specific situations. These international groups brought together people from different theological traditions and from different economic systems, which forced them to establish new ways of thinking together as Christians.

In writing about these studies David Jenkins rejected pure inductive and deductive models, which might be called 'linear', in favour of a circular process, basically but not wholly contextual in its method. In 'Concerning Theological Reflection' he argued that while we should recognize the necessary differences between theological discussion, political discussion, and engagement in some specific issue, we should also see them as parts of an organic whole, interacting with each other[8] (see diagram below).

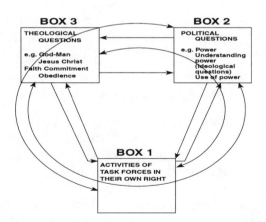

from Concerning Theological Reflection *by David Jenkins.*

7.   *Industrial Mission—An Appraisal*, p. 42.
8.   D.E. Jenkins, *Concerning Theological Reflection* (World Council of Churches Study Encounter, 7.3; Geneva: WCC, 1971).

This model suggested that one way to 'Do Theology' was to move from secular experience via political questions to the theological tradition and finally back to the secular situation but to seeing it in a new light.

The Development of the Model
Such a construct may be fine for those with David Jenkins's gifts, but how can Industrial Mission staff and their allies in the industrial world put this into practice?

Ian Fraser, who was Director of Studies at the Selly Oak Colleges in the 1970s developed a model for doing so and in June 1979 ran a course for Industrial Mission staff. Over a period of four days they applied an early version to the story of the Lucas Aerospace Combine Committee's Plan for Alternative Products. The acid test came on the last day when the output of intense deliberation by the group was reported back to some members of the Combine Committee. They were deeply interested and said that they had seen aspects of their work in a new light and that some very interesting new questions had been raised.

Fraser's arguments for seeking a new way of doing theology and his current version of the model are set out in *Reinventing Theology as the People's Work*.[9] There are some small differences between the model described here and that in the 1988 revision of the book.

The first major outing for the model in its Industrial Mission form was in a day conference for industrial relations practitioners organized by the Hertfordshire and Bedfordshire Industrial Mission in May 1981. This used an industrial relations case study as input. The model has been refined in a number of ways since, and used in a variety of settings.

The Application of the Model

This paper reports specifically on the use of this model in the induction course for new full time Industrial Mission staff, organized by the Industrial Mission Association and the William Temple Foundation. Each year the two tutors, Mike West and Malcolm Brown, have taken a group of about 12 participants through this exercise, in order to introduce them to theological methods in Industrial Mission. During this period the same method and case study have also been used with other groups of ministers in training programmes organized by IMSY.

9.   I.M. Fraser, *Reinventing Theology as the People's Work* (n.p.: Wild Goose, 3rd edn, 1988).

The current version of the brief introduction to and instructions for the method are in Appendix 1. Participants follow a case study, and are asked to imagine that they are invited as Industrial Mission staff to work with some of the characters in the story. They are provided with a one page summary of the 20 minutes programme; a full script is available.

The case study, a video of a BBC business programme, tells the story of the take over of Wordplex, a small British computer company by Norsk Data, a larger Norwegian business. Although its product was good, the financial and general management was weak and the after sales service inadequate. The video studies the period before and after the take over, which included the integration of the two companies on the new owner's site, and many redundancies. Some Wordplex staff rose to the top of the joint business, some left for new jobs, others became unemployed.

It has proved to be an ideal case study for this purpose. It is a sufficiently complex story to leave many judgments open for different interpretations. It uses industrial chaplains' interest in business matters, but does not assume too much technical knowledge.

The Process
The process is in five stages:

1. Identify the most significant themes in the story.
2. Select a manageable number of these themes.
3. For each theme, list
   a. the powers at work in it;
   b. the human consequences.
4. Identify biblical and theological resources relevant to the most significant powers and human consequences.
5. Apply this material to the original situation.

1. *Identify the most significant themes in the story.* This is more complex than it appears. Several different words have been tried to suggest ways of breaking down the situation into different aspects, without making premature ethical or political judgments. At times we have referred to 'elements', 'aspects' or 'issues'. Fraser uses 'crucial points'. 'Theme' seems to work best, as it retains the emphasis on the narrative and helps avoid premature judgments.

Many of our groups have struggled at this stage. They are clearly not used to systematic social analysis. For this reason, and to compress the time needed, we have suggested these themes for the group to work on:

a. changing company culture
b. what does it mean to 'manage people'?
c. buying and selling companies; the meaning of ownership
d. loaded language (eg: 'deadwood' = 'people')
e. corporate planning in an uncertain climate.

2. *Select a manageable number of these themes.* We have usually divided the group into two or three teams, each working on a single theme. Their selection in part reflects individuals' interests and experience. It also depends on the dynamics within the group, as does the whole process.

3. *For each theme list: a. the powers at work in it; b. the human consequences.* These are the 'political questions' in Jenkins' model. Here lies the particular feature of this model. In order to bridge the gap between the tradition and the industrial realities we use words which have a currency in both the industrial situation and in the tradition— although not necessarily the same currency. In this way the results of the 'political' stage are immediately usable in stage 4, identifying the relevant resources in the tradition.

The use of 'powers at work' can be seen clearly in Paul's cosmology and his proclamation of the universality of Christ, in Colossians 1.16 and 2.10. 'Every power and authority in the universe is subject to Christ.' This mythical explanation of the forces in the physical and social world is not so far from our use of ideas such as: 'market forces', 'racism' or 'imperialism'. Here are examples of powers at work identified by our groups: market forces, ownership, survival instinct, greed, self interest, paternalism, fear of change, the power of information.

The same is true of the use of 'human consequences' as a way of analysing the situation. There is a strong strand in the tradition, often in tension with other kinds of judgment, that measures human actions by the effects on people. We might justify this by reference to the Sheep and the Goats: 'whatever you did/did not to one of these, however insignificant, you did to me' (Mt. 25.40, 45). This use of a human measure, rather than economic or physical statistics, is common in current discussions of different political and economic systems. Here are examples of human consequences identified by our groups: uncertainty/false certainty, stress, changes in morale, inter-group resentment, groups gaining and groups suffering, disruption and growth.

Although there is always some discussion about what is meant by powers and consequences, most groups enjoy this stage in the process and are able to produce lists of ten or more in each category. Again, in order to compress the whole process into a working day, the teams are asked to choose the two or three most significant in each list to work on in the next stage.

4. *Identify biblical and theological resources relevant to the most significant powers and human consequences.* By this point the case study has been left behind, and the groups are working with lists of powers and human consequences, as generalities. The usual method of seeking biblical and theological resources is for the group to brainstorm possible material, and then to work over the list using all their critical faculties so that there is a minimum of misuse of texts!

The majority of members of these groups were ministers who have had a formal theological education. They find this stage fairly easy. When the model was used with a group of industrial relations specialists, as part of a study of participation in the workplace, they floundered. Their biblical knowledge is not just limited; it is not organized in ways which they can use for this purpose. In Fraser's version of the model, stages 1, 2 and 3 are undertaken by lay groups ('the people's work') and 'at this point, if so desired, there can be a significant use of theological experts who have up until then remained outside the process'.[10] Appendix 2 contains a detailed example.

5. *Apply this material to the original situation.* Here are examples of the applications produced by our groups:

> (to Norsk Data) what are your responsibilities to the workforce when you buy a company?
> (to the new management in Norsk) remember how little security you have had in this company when you deal with your subordinates.
> (to redundant workers) what have you actually lost by losing your job; what have you learned in the process?
> try to find ways that you can still use your skills, those you used when you worked for Wordplex, and those that were ignored.
> (to everyone) what is the nature of the employment relationship?
> is there a need for those currently successful to be reconciled to (and thus forgiven by) those who lost out in the take over.

---

10. Fraser, *Reinventing Theology*, p. 70.

Evaluation of the Method

For Industrial Mission staff the primary question will always be: Can we return to the problem with new ways of seeing it and new possibilities for resolving it? For a wider evaluation of the method two further questions might be asked: Are the new possibilities consistent with the Christian claim that 'Jesus is Lord'? Does the experience of the process, including the return to the situation, help add to the tradition in ways that extend and deepen it?

I suggest that the results outlined above, and those in other uses of the model, do create helpful new insights into the situation. I believe that this is a result of the use of biblical and theological tradition. Critics might say that it is just a complex way of standing back from the situation and seeing it from unexpected angles. To resolve this, the way in which the particular elements of the tradition are chosen and applied must be studied more exactly. That needs the attention of academic theologians.

I believe that the latter two questions above are easier to answer. The experience does give participants a revived sense that 'God is not dead, but busy in the impossible task of bringing in the Kingdom' and a commitment to finding ways of bridging the gaps between situations and tradition. The Fraser model is sufficiently powerful and well-founded to be usable in a variety of ways. It would be good if it could be used more widely, and further analysis made of its features—not least of the use of 'powers at work' and 'human consequences' as the key bridges between situation and tradition.

Appendix 1

Doing Theology

Inductive theology begins with our secular experience and explores its depths until the presence of the living God is uncovered. But every description and analysis we use is already infected by the presuppositions of the culture they come from, for us a competitive, secular culture.

Deductive theology begins with our inheritance from previous generations of Christians, and seeks to apply those general truths to our situation. But much of that tradition (at least the better known parts) is individualistic, sexist and imperialistic.

Most of the more helpful models of 'Doing Theology' developed by Urban and Industrial Mission teams combine elements of each in an attempt to avoid the worst features of both. We shall follow a method first developed by Dr Ian Fraser. He explains this method in *Reinventing Theology as the Peoples' Work.*

The Fraser Process

1. Identify and list the most significant *themes* in the story, avoiding premature ethical and political judgements.
2. Choose a manageable number of these themes.
3. For each theme list
   a. the powers at work in it, both personal and structural.
   b. the major human consequences.
4. a. for *each of the Powers* (or in the limited time the top two or three) identify relevant Biblical and theological resources. (It may be helpful to brainstorm possibly relevant material, then review the list in a more critical way.) How do these insights help understand each Power, and how we might respond to it?
   b. similarly for *each human consequence* (or at least the top three) list the relevant Biblical and theological material)
5. *Apply this* Biblical and theological material to the original situation.

For today please complete Stages 1, 2, 3 by 1245
4 by 1745
5 by 2015
and report your conclusions (Stage 5) on a flip chart sheet.

What alternative lines of thought and action do they suggest?
Imagine that one or more of the main characters belongs to an Industrial Mission Study group and asked for your comments.

> The OT is about persons and communities moving under God, saying 'yes' and 'no' to him concerning the way they manage their personal and communal life on a large canvas of the clash of nations and the rise and fall of kingdoms. The NT is about one who 'fills the universe' affecting it at every point in its complexity; and about a new community which exists to be a foretaste to the whole household of humankind of a fuller life in store for us, a life marked by justice and peace. (Ian Fraser).

Appendix 2

One group chose to work on the theme: 'What does it mean to "manage people" in this context?' They identified many powers at work and human consequences, and then focused on two powers:

the drive for efficiency through cost cutting
the pressure to change

and three consequences:

decline in loyalty
new physical environments
insecurity

After their brainstorming session they listed these biblical resources:

Concerning the drive for efficiency through cost cutting: Falsifying scales in Amos; unjust steward; Paul's tentmaking ministry; making bricks without straw; Naboth's vineyard; disciples sent out without purse or spare shoes; Paul and the silversmiths; Jesus and the temple traders; pruning the vine for better fruit; David eating sanctuary bread.

Insecurity: Israelites in Babylon—'sing us the songs of Zion'; disciples after Jesus' arrest; division within families because of the faith; Peter walking (or rather not walking) on the water; early Church meeting behind closed doors

THE ENTERPRISE CULTURE[*]

Peter Sedgwick

In the 1980s a change came over English cultural life. Throughout much of the post-war period the commitment to full employment by politicians reflected a determination never to repeat the horrors of the long depression of the 1930s. As William Haley wrote, 'Jarrow bit more deeply into the British memory than the Somme, even more deeply than Hitler was to do'.[1] Haley argued that throughout the post-war period after 1945 there was a defensive national attitude, a jealousy of class domination and inherited wealth, strengthened by years of frustration and hardship. Alongside that attitude there was a failure to treat trades unions in a responsible way, with a reciprocal suspicion of management by the unions; a sterile political debate where each party sought to undo the gains of the other; and the growth of a welfare state, which became massively over-centralized. Perhaps the most acute critic here was David Donnison, who himself directed the Supplementary Benefits Commission. He saw in the increasing standardization, regimentation and disregard for particular needs a 'monument to the labours of blinkered men'.[2] Finally there was the dead hand of status and class, where deference to the upper classes permeated much of English life, in particular, before 1939. This died slowly after 1945, but it was not until the 1960s that class seemed to be no longer the dominant feature of English society, even if it was still prevalent in many areas.

In the 1960s to the 1980s, a period of great uncertainty was evident in British culture. Gradually more of the middle-class was made up of those

---

[*]   Given as the Basingstoke and North Hampshire Industrial Mission Inaugural Award Lecture, 13 October 1993.

1.   W. Haley, review of R.R. James, *The British Revolution*, in *The Times*, 1976 (no date).

2.   D. Donnison, *Urban Policy: A New Approach* (Fabian Pamphlet 487; London: Fabian Society, 1983), and *idem*, *The Times*, 4 March 1983.

born into the working-class. It was a time of fierce industrial action, social and geographical mobility and the rejection of much of the welfare state as heavy handed and paternalistic. The mid 1970s in particular saw high inflation, the impact of worldwide competition, a rise in unemployment, new technology and (in the personal sphere) the exploration of new moral attitudes. By 1980, the government in power had decided on an open espousal of the market as the solution to Britain's industrial and political problems. At the same time, however, there was increasingly a rejection by young people, and others, of a lifetime spent working in a hierarchical organization, where one slowly moved up the ladder until one reached one's limit.

Professor Allan Gibb, at Durham University Business School, has created an enterprise/education unit within the Business School which is remarkably successful. He argues that many schools and higher education institutions did not see themselves as facilitating innovation, but only as promoting a narrow range of skills. The other main constraint was the fear of failure, where schools insisted that information was received and little responsibility was given to pupils. This is not an attack on teachers, who do an excellent job in the present climate, but rather to suggest that education was orientated for decades toward producing the conformist, essentially reactive, academic person that society required, or else turned out the ill-equipped 'hand' to work at a low-skill, manual job in a steel works, or other heavy industrial employer. It was the reaction against this which created an interest in self-employment, creativity and enterprise.

It is therefore important to realize that the exploration of enterprise involves participative education. In some primary schools this flourished thirty years ago, although the impoverishment of the surrounding area meant that it was difficult to translate this into concrete results in the world after school. Nor should it be assumed that the commitment to the market is the same as the exploration of enterprise. Clearly they can be equated, as in the strong promotion of self-employment by the Conservative government in the 1980s. But a more profound analysis will see them both as challenging the older British culture of low expectation, gradual change and great reliance on institutional life. The market put such institutions into a cauldron of consumer driven choices, often to quite disastrous effect in the case of education. But sometimes it did make bureaucracies more responsive to the world outside them. However this is not my concern in this article: consideration of the market's role in health, education or the mass media is too vast a topic to consider here. (Andrew Britton has an article in *Crucible* January 1993 on health and education[3]). What I wish to point to is the cultural expectation of many people that they no longer had to work within the world of great institutions, and that such institutions, from British Leyland to the National Health Service, were becoming more fragmented, smaller, and facing rapid change. Perhaps there was somewhere else where one could work. This takes me to entrepreneurship.

Entrepreneurship is classically defined by Joseph Schumpeter, the Austrian economist who worked in the United States. He wrote in 1943 of the 'perennial gale of creative destruction' that is the paradox of modern economic life. As more inventions come into existence, new technology, new commodities, new organizations all destroy existing firms and their very lives. It is salutary to remember at the end of a recession that has claimed so many jobs and so many firms' very existence that Schumpeter pointed out that the greatest destruction of jobs is in times of prosperity. With prosperity come new innovations that revolutionize the existing economic order. The classic paradigm of course is the steam train, which destroyed stage coaches and horse wagons in under two decades. Schumpeter argues that it was not merely new products, but new technology, organizations and marketing that could, separately or together, destroy an old order by making it obsolete. But only a few people can act in this way. To quote Schumpeter directly, the entrepreneur has a task which lies

> outside the routine tasks which everybody understands and...the environment resists in many ways... To act with confidence beyond the range of familiar beacons and to overcome that resistance requires aptitudes that are present in only a small fraction of the population.[4]

If you define enterprise in this way, it is not the same necessarily as a small business. A small business, like a large one, may be profoundly conservative, and offer, say, the same painting and decorating business handed on from generation to generation in a family firm for decades. But a small firm at least has the potential for rapid innovation which is more difficult for the larger one. Charles Handy, the eminent management theorist, has drawn attention in recent years to growing devolution

---

3.   A. Britton, 'Patients and Pupils, Customers and Clients: Quasi Markets in Health and Education', *Crucible* (Jan. 1993).

4.   J. Schumpeter, *Capitalism, Socialism and Democracy* (London: Harper & Row, 1943), pp. 83 and 132-33.

among large firms, so that with devolution of power and responsibility, innovation might become easier.[5] This is sometimes called 'intrepreneurship'. Nevertheless, much of the innovation in recent years in sectors such as electronics has come from people leaving large corporations and setting up on their own precisely to encourage innovation and change. Innovation has also come in community ventures.

Enterprise then consists of entrepreneurial behaviour. It is self-reliant, innovating, risk-taking and thrives upon the devolution of responsibility. The most crucial fact to note is that entrepreneurs are made and not born. Those who seek innovation and risk-taking have complex motives. Creativity, initiative taking, high autonomy and leadership are all aspects of an entrepreneur. But they may stem from an inadequate personality, who can only exist in a restless search for self-justification; and a person who is a workaholic driving subordinates to infantile behaviour patterns. Or they may reflect the drive for greater personal independence, extraordinary determination and sheer physical energy. It is crucial that people feel challenged, seeking to explore new opportunities. Thus those who have studied such people speak of the 'entrepreneurial decision'. It may be the nineteen year old setting up a tie-die printing workshop for T-shirts; or, in the complex world of management consultancy, leaving a large firm and setting up on one's own. It may be community enterprise, seeking a new way to build one's own house, or the failing engineering firm where there is a management buy-out. In each case, here is entrepreneurial behaviour, which has to be self-reliant, innovative and risk-taking, in combination with an entrepreneurial decision.

An enterprise culture is thus an umbrella term for a whole series of different decisions, and may in fact almost be a meaningless phrase. What unites a Somali restaurant in East London with a hi-tech science laboratory at Warwick University Science Park? Very little indeed. But when a culture changes, then the relevant attributes in a young person can be significantly affected. I believe that despite the hype associated with Lord Young and the Thatcher government in the mid-1980s, a change began to be discernible among those under 40, and more especially those leaving school. Role models were created: the first initiative by a group of women, the first small business or co-operative. Repeated social surveys in the late 1980s suggested that this change was much greater than government persuasion might be responsible for. Nor was it necessarily associated with views hostile to the welfare state. Peter Kellner,

5.   C. Handy, *The Age of Unreason* (London: Business Books, 1989).

a political journalist, noticed that 'Thatcher's children' were far more prepared to set up on their own in business, in co-operatives or in community enterprise than their parents' generation were, but equally were more in favour of comprehensives, the National Health Service, and racial equality.[6] Perhaps, then, there is no such thing as an 'enterprise culture': it sounds suspiciously like a Department of Trade and Industry initiative. What certainly exists is a series of cultures which separately exemplify entrepreneurial behaviour. These are the youth cultures of the North and South, with significant regional differences; ethnic, male, female, service, managerial and community cultures. They are not all to be admired. Some of the research shows a world of long hours, low salaries and high insecurity for the hundredth hairdresser to set up as an alternative to unemployment on a poor Cleveland housing estate (I have visited some myself). But this anticipates the more detailed survey which follows. Before outlining this, however, it is important to make one final point. There is also an anti-entrepreneurial culture, where self-reliance, risk and innovation are regarded as inimical. It is sobering to find Charles Handy, and others from management, regarding institutional religion as exemplifying in this century a profoundly anti-entrepreneurial culture.

Trevor MacDonald wrote from the world of management:

> The Church, in its secular manifestation, with its structures, hierarchy, committees, and formalised consultative processes, is an institution par excellence. To that extent, as much contemporary evidence demonstrates, it is very difficult, particularly for those integral to its organization, to have an appreciation or sympathy for the enterprise culture.[7]

One of the most obvious aspects of entrepreneurship is Asian enterprise, caught better perhaps in the film *My Beautiful Launderette* than in the stereotype of the corner shopkeeper. Gradually less of the effort of the Asian community is going into shopkeeping, although it remains an important area. Black-led training programmes such as Full Employ took 1000 government-funded places in the 1980s. Individuals such as Nazmu Virani have expanded dramatically into hotels and pubs, while others work in public relations, journalism and manufacturing. Much of this effort reflected a determination to resist racial prejudice. In a similar way, women turned to running firms for themselves. There was a 70%

---

6. P. Kellner, *The Independent*, 15 August 1988.
7. T. MacDonald; letter to author in P. Sedgwick, *The Enterprise Culture* (London: SPCK, 1992).

rise in female self-employment from 1981–87. Many women in the Department of Employment surveys spoke of deciding to work for themselves after meeting a lack of comprehension among male managers. More positively, there was a desire for independence, often after a difficult period in their lives. To quote the Department of Employment report directly:

> A major difference between male and female owned businesses lies in the criteria upon which success is judged. Women generally regarded success in terms of how well the business met individual needs rather than in conventional terms of profitability and income gained.[8]

Community enterprise can be a financial service providing revolving loans within a community, or can own and develop community resources such as land, buildings or equipment. The Church of England promoted a scheme called Linking-Up to relate ventures in different cities to one another. 'It is there to generate income in a local community and to prevent outflow: community businesses, enterprises, credit unions.' Alongside this there is the development of co-operatives, which combine the virtues of self-reliance and risk-taking with those of mutual support, decision making and profit-sharing. There is also the dimension of enterprise education already referred to, at Durham and elsewhere. Here the emphasis is not on starting businesses, but on self-reliance and initiative. Theologically the enterprise culture can be evaluated in two different ways. There is the view of Bishop David Jenkins, formerly of Durham, who denounces it as manifesting the greed, competition and lack of compassion so common in the culture of an advanced, Western industrialized society. While his talks on the enterprise culture remain, so far as I know, unpublished, there are his addresses published in 1988 as *God, Politics and the Future*.[9] The market is his central concern, and he sees it as promoting gross inequality, exploitation and a rate of growth which is unsustainable. Idolatry and the treatment of the poor provoke the sharpest denunciations of the Old Testament prophets. Jenkins argues that idolatry 'is manifested by many ways of commitment to the piling up of wealth—the irresponsible enjoyment of luxury...self-indulgence and sensuousness'.[10]

8.   S. Carter and T. Cannon, *Female Entrepreneurs*, Department of Employment Research Paper No. 65.

9.   D.E. Jenkins, *God, Politics and the Future* (London: SCM Press, 1983).

10. Jenkins, *God, Politics and the Future*, p. 51.

Certainly the enterprise culture has provided many examples of greed and exploitation. However, many of those whom I interviewed in the research which formed the basis for my book, *The Enterprise Culture*, did not place a desire for wealth as their sole objective. Instead there was a search for values, which they could no longer express where they worked. Common values which they articulated were those of creativity, community and freedom. The theological challenge is to seek to strengthen the social relationships which exist between people. Freedom in relationship to community encompasses both new forms of social order and new expressions of personal meaning. I have found the Roman Catholic theologian Karl Rahner helpful in elucidating this dimension of human life. Rahner's argument is that in the ongoing search for personal responsibility and commitment, transcendence is not the experience of some definite, objective thing. It is a mode of existence and a way of living prior to every existence. Transcendence offers a person the choice of free action. Whether the freedom that is expressed in, say, the decision to be self-employed is seen as a gift and as something which one receives, becomes the religious question. So transcendence for a Christian refers to the ultimate mystery and freedom of a person's openness, and to the ground of that freedom in the absolute mystery called God. That does not mean that the search for new values must be religious. It is only implicitly so. Nevertheless, the decision for self-employment or community enterprises, is not to be equated in itself with greed. And transcendence can lead into the experience of God.

As the decade reached its end, it became clear that the government had seriously mismanaged the economy. Instead of the government assisting the growth of enterprise, the rapid fiscal tightening and worsening balance of payments crisis led to a collapse in the whole culture of small firms, self-employment and co-operatives. Firms that grew on government contracts, or sub-contracting, found their very existence at stake.

What future, then, remains for the enterprise culture after the disasters of the years 1989–92? In October 1991 Dunn and Bradsheet reported a 71% rise in business failures so far that year, the highest rise since records began in 1980.[11] Thirty-three thousand companies failed in 9 months, investment by small firms was at the lowest level for 6 years, and business purchases dropped by 50%. The figures however should not deflect our attention from the fundamental changes which happened in the 1980s. The proportion of self-employed people rose from 7.9% in

11. Dunn and Bradsheet survey in *The Times*, October 1991 (no date).

1980 to 12.3%. By 1986 23% of the UK workforce was in companies employing less than 10 workers, and 47% in companies employing 10–499 workers. This is now significantly higher than Germany, where only 27% work in medium-sized companies (under 499 workers), and 18% work in companies employing under 10 workers. These figures were not much reduced by the 1989–92 recession.

Outside of central and local government employment, the number working in small firms employing under 20 workers rose from 27% of the workforce in 1979, to 35% in 1989. The problem now is the financing of small firms; and there has been a continual criticism of the high street banks. Unlike the German government, which set up an institution to lend to small businesses 40 years ago at only 0.5% above base rates, the British government puts its faith in the job creation prospects of small firms, while allowing them to pay up to 9% above base rates on the open market.

There have been wide variations in survival rates. In a recent survey of London small businesses, 24% of clothing firms survived the decade 1979–89; 35% in toys; 79–82% in electronics and pharmaceuticals; 86% in printing. Equally, size was a feature in survival. For businesses in existence in 1979, only 50% of those employing less than 10 in London survived by 1989, but 66% of those employing more than 20 were still there. Equally, long-established businesses fare better than those with only a few years of life behind them.

So it seems that a sizeable number of small businesses have not only survived, but will prosper. Indeed, Professor Gallagher of Newcastle University has shown nationally that in the years immediately before the recession 93,000 firms employing 1–4 people were responsible for no less than half the total gross job creation, and firms employing under ten people created over half the total net new jobs of 520,000 workers. (Net jobs are the balance between job losses and job creations; gross jobs simply defines new jobs.) Of course, the moral case against the creation of small firms which sub-contract from larger firms and only survive by paying very low wages, especially to women and in bad conditions, remains very strong indeed. Nevertheless, the innovative style created by small firms will outlast this recession, even if their growth is slower than in the 1980s. The moral question remains the nature and conditions of employment in small firms. There are wide variations on this.

The problem for the 1990s is no longer the creation of an enterprise culture, but the persistence and deepening of long-term unemployment.

It is striking that in my former city of Hull, the city council is now experimenting with a whole range of options to break long-term male unemployment. Local exchange transfer systems are a way of trading without currency; credit unions and wholesale co-operatives involve the community; and a group of workshops now exists on an outer estate with management by those from the estate itself. Clearly small businesses on their own are not going to reverse the rising trend of unemployment. As with the market, the question of full employment is too large a topic to give extensive consideration to here. However Frank Field (MP) has linked a commitment to full employment with a desire to sustain individual initiatives in self-employment.[12]

It seems likely that unemployment will remain high for some years, if not indefinitely. Larger firms will continue to shed labour, and the only possibility of job creation is by much greater training and the active intervention of the government. Within that the role of small firms remains crucial. CBI surveys show that small firms are beginning to lead the country out of recession. Yet simply taking an economic analysis will not do justice to the profound changes which the enterprise culture has wrought in our society. Ultimately the enterprise culture was more than an economic change: it was a cultural one.

We are faced with a profound theological question. The Commission on Social Justice puts it like this in their second booklet, *Social Justice in a Changing World*:

> The welfare state...failed to make citizens feel it was theirs...individual problems were to be solved by experts and there were few, if any mechanisms for ordinary people to participate in decisions affecting their own lives... Greater personal independence, paradoxically, means increasing social independence... The challenge to the Commission is to develop new mechanisms of collective action which will at the same time meet common goals and liberate individual talent.[13]

How should individual talent be liberated in a society where common goals become increasingly difficult to define, let alone realize? The answer may lie in the relationship of love to justice. Self-denial is an impossible, undesirable ideal, however much it may have featured in the Christian tradition. The conscious attempt to renounce self leads to the renouncer becoming bound up with his or her own self. So self-valuing becomes

---

12. F. Field, *Losing Out* (London: Blackwell Books, 1989).

13. Commission on Social Justice Discussion Paper 2, *Social Justice in a Changing World* (July 1993), pp. 20-21.

significant, and a proper liberation of talent will include that. Those who have found fulfilment in community enterprise, small businesses and co-operatives often remember the risks, pain and sometimes complete collapse which such ventures bring. But if there is success then there is an affirmation of self, which can lead the person out into the love of others and regard for their worth too. Certainly that is the experience of many who were successful in the 1980s, and also would never seek to go back to an older, more regimented existence. But two questions remain, and they are pressing. One is to ask what sense such reflections make for those who continue to work within institutions, where the pace of change is rapid and unremitting. It is no part of my brief to disparage large institutions, but rather to raise questions which one part of our culture must put to another. (It is interesting that David Jenkins will be working after his retirement on the problems of institutions in the modern world.) The other is one which must be answered—the question of justice. Michael Walzer in *Spheres of Justice* links justice to self-respect and autonomy.[14] Self-respect depends on owning our actions and our lives. We are responsible for what we do, we hold ourselves responsible and others hold us responsible. Distributive justice, which distributes wealth and opportunity (including education) to all members of a society, makes self-respect possible. It does not guarantee it, but it enables the minimum of self-respect to exist. Self-respect and autonomy are integral to the themes of freedom and creativity which I have sought to address.

That is why a welfare state remains, and must remain, the foundation for establishing a welfare state which enables self-respect, and so entrepreneurial behaviour. But that is only the first step for justice. Responsibility to others is the final claim which God lays on us, for freedom only consists in responsibility, and responsibility presupposes freedom. Bonhoeffer pointed out that responsibility goes beyond simply the challenge of making decisions. Responsibility is in vocation and relationships. So this consideration of enterprise leaves us with the question of how relationships may be developed in this town which take responsibility for its life. I return to the issues with which I began, such as defensive national attitudes, suspicion and the search for a viable way forward. Only now we are in the 1990s, not in the period 1945–79. Our society is more fragmented, and the weight of the past is less heavy: there is more opportunity for self-expression, but is there less opportunity for service to the

14. M. Walzer, *Spheres of Justice* (New York: Basic Books, 1983), p. 279.

community? It is these questions which I leave you with as the 'enterprise culture' itself becomes part of British social and economic history.

In conclusion, I have tried to present a picture of British life which some may find controversial. Analysing our society before 1939, and for much of the period after it, there was alongside the compassion, tolerance and solidarity a great deal of restraint on people's freedom to choose their own lives. In the 1980s this restraint burst, and the enterprise culture came into existence. It can be seen as greed and as naked individualism; but there was also much creativity and self- expression. It is not in itself a religious movement at all, but again and again in my interviews I found people seeking to articulate the meaning of their search for freedom and creativity in ways which the churches could answer, if they wished. Ironically the government which sought to promote it ended up by damaging it deeply. Nevertheless, the cultural change has taken place, leaving us with questions of justice, and responsibility, in the confusing world of British society today.

THE IMPLICATIONS OF THE NEW SCIENTIFIC WORLDVIEW
FOR THEOLOGY TODAY

John David Weaver

Introduction

The modern popularity of science is evidenced by the plethora of books dealing with human life and the universe. The interest in these books reflects the modern concern with questions of the origins, purpose and meaning of life. The growth of the Green Movement and New Age religion can also be seen as part of this search, with the central concerns for the environment of the planet, and the use of resources, together with monistic beliefs in a world soul, and the interconnectedness of human life with the whole of the cosmos.

Science is presenting an ever clearer picture of the universe of which we are a part. We are understanding more and more of the complex patterns and structures of the galaxies, of human life and of the sub-atomic particles that compose all things. Cosmologists speak of the discovery of design and pose questions about purpose. There is a growing weight of evidence to suggest that human life could only have developed on this planet through a unique set of parameters, which were established at the birth of the universe itself. The fragile conditions that enabled life to develop are now seen to be adversely affected by human activity, leading to the pollution of the environment, the exhaustion of natural resources and the destruction of the protective ozone layer. With the same anthropocentric attitude that led to the present state of affairs, people are seeking to solve the world's scientifically discovered problems through lobbying of governments and through legislation, most of which is beneficial to the rich nations, but takes little account of the 'four-fifths' world.

The history of the universe, being discovered by modern cosmology, is pointing to a God who does not work by magic, but who has been patiently at work, over a long period of time, in an evolving universe.

Science presents us with a universe that has a beginning and which will have a definite end, in which carbon-based life will be extinguished. Theology attempts to pull together the whole of human experience, physical, mental, emotional and spiritual, producing a holistic view of the universe in which we exist. Theology hears the questions raised by the fine-tuning of the universe and sees within it the hand of God described at the beginning of Scripture.

There is a limit to how far science can ever take us in our understanding of the world in which we live. The former NASA astrophysicist, Robert Jastrow, was probably correct in his assessment:

> For the scientist who has lived by his faith in the power of reason, the story ends like a bad dream. He has scaled the mountains of ignorance; he is about to conquer the highest peak; and as he pulls himself over the final rock, he is greeted by a band of theologians who have been sitting there for centuries.[1]

In my own work[2] I have sought to address the theological issues that are raised by modern science, concluding that

> Science asks why the universe displays purpose, and looks for a theory of everything. We are able to point the world to the Creator who is the author of life, and whose ultimate purpose is declared in the life, death and resurrection of Christ. Science points to the anthropocentric nature of the universe, and asks what this might mean. We are able to point to the Creator who has created human beings in his own image. Ordinary people ask about origins, purpose, meaning, and suffering, and we are able to engage them with the realities of the scientific understanding of the world, and thereby to lead them deeper into the truth of God revealed in Christ.[3]

Enlightenment Worldview

There has been a revolution in our understanding of the physical world over the last 300 years. Copernicus and Galileo pointed us to a universe that was not centred on Earth; and Kepler and Newton pointed us toward the physical laws by which the universe operated. For Newton

---

1. R.D. Jastrow, *Reader's Digest* (October 1980), p. 57, quoted in D. Wilkinson, *God, the Big Bang and Stephen Hawking* (Tunbridge Wells: Monarch, 1993), p. 71.

2. J. Weaver, *In the Beginning God—Modern Science and the Christian Doctrine of Creation* (Macon, Smyth and Helwys; Oxford: Regent's Park College, 1994).

3. Weaver, *In the Beginning God*, pp. 200-201

God was not at the centre, but outside, holding the whole dynamic system within a timeless and motionless framework. Newton thought of the universe as the rational design of God, with its infinite size related to the all-embracing Spirit of God. Newton's work both affirmed God and at the same time limited what he could be and do. The possibility of miracles, revelation or intervention by God was not possible within a universe governed by natural laws. A new meta-narrative was born and here was laid the basis of a dualism between religious experience and the scientific observation of nature, which is still with us.

Palaeontologists and biologists have discovered an enormous diversity in living organizms. Darwin proposed natural selection to account for the development, variety and complexity of living things; Mendel, and later Crick and Watson, through their work in the field of genetics, showed the biological mechanism by which evolution might occur. Richard Dawkins denies that the evolution of complex life forms indicates purpose, but we must question whether this denial can be sustained with regard to the human mind.[4] In a fascinating study of the mind, Roger Penrose suggests that consciousness appears to be the element in the brain which allows us to see and appreciate what mathematical truth is, and this in itself demonstrates that the brain is not a computer.[5] We might add to this the perception of aesthetic beauty in art, music and nature, or the emotions of hope, fear, anxiety or despair. Penrose concludes with these remarks: 'Consciousness seems to me to be such an important phenomenon that I cannot believe that it is something just "accidently" conjured up by a complicated computation. It is the phenomenon whereby the universe's very existence is made known.'[6] Even though much of what is involved in mental activity might work in the same way as a computer, the conscious mind itself cannot do so.

The Darwinian concept of evolution presented a picture of life getting better and better, and raised the possibility of human self-determinism. This thinking was taken up as social darwinism first by Marx and then more extremely by Hitler. Life in the hands of what the biological sciences can achieve has led to the ethical problems highlighted in the debate over eggs taken from the ovaries of an aborted foetus being implanted into an infertile woman. But while some biologists are moving towards a

4.   R. Dawkins, *The Blind Watchmaker* (London: Longmans, 1986).
5.   R. Penrose, *The Emperor's New Mind* (Oxford: Oxford University Press, 1989).
6.   Penrose, *The Emperor's New Mind*, p. 447

hard materialism, physicists faced with compelling experimental evidence have been moving away from strictly mechanical models of the universe to a view that sees the mind playing an integral role in all physical events. There is a fascinating irony here in that biologists who ought to be dealing with questions of relationship and community among life forms are moving towards a hard materialistic view of life reduced to chemical reactions and physical equations, while cosmologists, who work with mathematical equations, are increasingly speaking about a 'purpose' that goes beyond equations.

Postmodernism: Removal of the Meta-Narratives

Modern industrial society has developed through an elitism based on meta-narratives, which emphasize the knowledge and causal processes of rationalism. This meta-narrative of modernity largely replaced the meta-narrative of the Christian faith or of any other faith system. With the collapse of this new 'faith' in the infallibility of science has come the postmodern disdain of elitism and of trust in the rational grand narrative. In discussing the rise of postmodernism, Philip Sampson says

> Postmodernism celebrates mass, popular culture over the elitist high culture of modernism; consumers over professionals; the citizen over the expert... Postmodernity reflects a loss of confidence in all the old certainties and justifications of Western society.[7]

He believes that there is a loss of confidence in the old certainties of science, medicine, law and education. Many Christians recognize postmodernism's rejection of arrogant and doctrinaire rationalism, while seeing the irrationalism that replaces it as even worse. They see the flourishing of New Age religion as the product of postmodernism—an eclectic conglomeration of beliefs, which pander to and are a product of the individualism and consumerism that has been the mark of a postmodern world.

But in recent years science, technology and industrial advances have had an increasingly bad press, and materialism has, for many people, been found to be an empty dream. The last decade has seen the flowering of a syncretism of a wide variety of non-Christian religions, often referred to collectively as 'New Age', and also a re-emergence of the older primal

7. P. Sampson, *The Rise of Postmodernity*, in P. Sampson, V. Samuel and C. Sugden (eds.), *Faith and Modernity* (Oxford: Regnum LYNX, 1994), p. 46

religions, which may be described as 'neo-paganism'. I consider that David Burnett is right to attribute the large appeal these have in *popular* culture to a relativistic secularism where the equal validity of all beliefs is readily accepted, and where people feel free to do whatever they consider to be right and to follow any course that leads to self advancement.[8] Behind the interest that many are showing in these movements is the search for an understanding of the world we experience and for our place within the scheme of things; there is a search for personal fulfilment and wellbeing.

We have the opportunity to present the gospel as the only foundation adequate to support the grand narratives which modernity took for granted. Tormod Engelsviken makes a similar point, noting that modernity has led to a widespread loss of meaning and purpose resulting from causal reasoning and a lack of teleological orientation. In the postmodern era nihilism seems to replace the grand narratives of modernity. But, says Engelsviken, people cannot and will not live without meaning and purpose.[9] Modern cosmology of Big Bang beginnings and a designer universe and Christian eschatology offer the meaning and purpose that society longs for.

New Cosmology—A New Meta-Narrative

Scientists such as Roger Penrose (Oxford), Stephen Hawking (Cambridge), Paul Davies (formerly Newcastle, now at the University of Adelaide) and John Barrow (University of Sussex) have devoted their attention to the nature of the beginning of the universe.[10] Einstein's General Theory of Relativity, the field of quantum physics and Heisenberg's Uncertainty Principle, researched at the beginning of this century, pointed away from an entirely predictable universe. Hubble in the 1920s had suggested that the universe was expanding, which implied a universe with a beginning, and the discovery in the 1960s of a cosmic heat radiation field supported the theory of a hot 'Big Bang' at the start

8.   D. Burnett, *Clash of Worlds* (Eastbourne: Monarch, 1990), p. 202.
9.   T. Engelsviken, *Modernity and Eschatology*, in Sampson, Samuel and Sugden (eds.), *Faith and Modernity*, p. 175.
10.   See J. Barrow, *Theories of Everything* (Oxford: Oxford University Press, 1990); P. Davies, *The Mind of God* (New York: Simon & Schuster, 1992); S. Hawking, *A Brief History of Time* (London: Bantum Press, 1988); Penrose, *The Emperor's New Mind*.

of it all. Scientists have discovered a uniformly expanding universe of great size and age: 100,000 billion, billion kilometres across and some 15-20 billion years old.

One of the greatest surprises is that the present state of the universe has depended on a 'fine tuning' of the initial conditions that brought it into existence. Modern cosmologists speak of an 'Anthropic Principle'. It is widely accepted that there is some guiding principle or even 'design' that has allowed complex human life to arise within the universe.

There is a paradigm shift in worldview demonstrated here. The scientific thought of the eighteenth and nineteenth centuries saw a universe that was infinite and was progressing to a better future.[11] The universe was seen as an orderly, predictable system, strictly materialistic. Now the Anthropic Principle that appears to be woven into its fabric, and the non-algorithmic nature of the human mind, which suggests the special nature of homo sapiens, have all sought to give planet Earth a central place in the apparently purposeful evolution of the universe. The key change that has been brought about by modern cosmological research is the suggestion of *purpose*. This must lead inevitably to a paradigm shift in the scientific and secular world-views held by many people outside the Church. But for all this talk of design and purpose, these scientists would all agree that to speak of design is a scientific conclusion, while to speak of a designer would be a matter of personal belief.

A universe which is not infinite, nor closed, nor entirely predictable, but which has purpose and is open to change, has room for faith to find God's immanence as well as God's transcendence. Human beings cannot be viewed as machines, as science has recognized the non-algorithmic nature of the mind and of personhood. There are perceptions that are not computable; and the universe seems to have evolved with human-kind having a central place. We must therefore question how we obtain information and knowledge, and we cannot see our own individualistic rights and needs as an end in themselves, because we appear to be a part of a cosmic plan. In short, in the modern scientific view of the world there is a place for the mystical, for a God who accompanies creation, and for an emphasis on our role as stewards. A concern for all human life must also become an essential element in our thinking, both economic and political.

John Polkinghorne is correct when he says, 'Religion without science

11. For use of the term 'paradigm shift', see T.S. Kuhn, *The Structure of Scientific Revolutions* (Chicago: Phoenix Books, 1962)

is confined; it fails to be completely open to reality'. But also, 'Science without religion is incomplete; it fails to attain the deepest possible understanding'.[12] The biblical account of creation presents important doctrinal statements concerning God's relationship with his creation. These statements are received by faith, and their reception is expressed in worship. The God of creation is also celebrated as the God of salvation, and the Father of our Lord Jesus Christ. He is the God who is manifest in the world through his Spirit, and who will bring the whole universe to its completion. For science the cosmic future is bleak, whether it consists of Heat Death or Big Crunch. What is true of the cosmos is true of humanity, ending in a death which shows the futility of life. There is no conflict between the Big Bang of modern cosmology and the biblical view of creation. But God is the God of creation, which is to be understood as his continuing act, leading towards the goal that he has purposed and promised.

Stewardship of Creation

Modern cosmology does not confirm a simple progressive view. It envisages an increasing entropy and so an increasing disorder, with a hostile end in a 'Big Crunch' or 'Heat Death'. We observe that the state of increasing entropy makes it possible for human beings, through their freedom of choice, to disturb the balance of nature with its finely tuned laws, so that tragedy results. The paradigm shift in worldview offers hope and choice to human beings. We have the knowledge and the understanding, which enable us to choose to be wise stewards of creation.

Within the contingency of nature suggested by science, there is room for the emergence of 'natural' evil due to the distortion of living organizms at microscopic levels. Science demonstrates that the same processes that gave rise to the evolution of human life, namely the mutation of genes, also lead to disease and death. This is to be understood in theological terms as the risk God takes in endowing creation with freedom. In individual cases of suffering we will still of course have to wrestle with the questions of healing and wholeness, alongside pain and grief. There is no simple rational formula that can be applied to dissolve the mystery. In the mystery of suffering we will need to hold onto the model of suffering love that we see displayed in the cross of Christ, where we find the creator suffering with and on behalf of the world.

12. J. Polkinghorne, *Science and Creation* (London: SPCK, 1988), p. 97.

The discoveries of science also allow us to tackle a very different kind of so-called 'natural evil', the suffering brought about by events in the physical world such as earthquakes, volcanic eruptions and extremes of climate. We recognize that these are necessary side effects of a world designed to produce the raw materials of life. Here it seems to me that we blame God too easily and too readily speak of these as 'evil' in themselves. Their disastrous nature actually mainly stems from the moral evil of human irresponsibility. With the help of modern science we are able to predict where and when disasters of this kind are likely to take place. So countries which are rich in resources and technology *could* counter such anticipated problems and avoid the worst effects if they had the will-power to accept the economic costs; for example, houses need not be built on a major fracture in Earth's crust in California, and farmers need not farm on the slopes of Mount Etna. Poorer countries cannot themselves take evasive action; they need help. Unless developed countries are willing to share their wealth, living space and expertise with others less advantaged, large populations will go on living, for example, on the coastal flood plains of Bangladesh. Thus, to raise the moral question of the goodness of God also involves a moral issue for us.

Human beings are created with the ability to control creation to some extent, with a freedom and power given to us by God. The question that remains will be our response. We are brought face to face once again with a God who, in self-limiting love, gives freedom of choice to his creation, and who himself lives with the consequences of such an action. We have clearly found the God of love, revealed in his creation and in the cross of Christ.

Conclusion

An expanding universe with a beginning and an end, exhibiting design and apparent purpose, is suggestive of God the creator. We have the revival of the teleological argument which poses the question, to which one answer may be God. Here is my apologetic to the postmodern world.

A universe which includes natural disasters, suffering and pollution, accords with being the creation of a self-limiting God, who gives choice to his creation. Here is my understanding of God who accompanies and suffers with his creation.

The paradigm shift in worldview from one of optimistic progress within an infinite cosmos to a model of a universe which moves from

Big Bang to Big Crunch or Heat Death, and in which there is a delicate balance both to produce and destroy life, forces us to consider carefully both our own future and our care of the planet. Here is my understanding of the place of humanity in creation, both *imago Dei* and as stewards of creation: A place of hope and choice for all people.

INDUSTRIAL CULTURE AND HUMAN VALUES

David McLellan

Is our society industrial or post-industrial? modern or postmodern? Whatever the answer to these questions, all would agree that there is *some* continuity.[1] Capitalist society has not transformed itself into something else. So I propose to outline the intellectual/cultural presuppositions of traditional industrial society before going on to discuss the recent changes which have led some to talk about a *post*-industrial society, and then to reflect on the kind of resources we possess to question and reform the offences to human values so evident in our dominant attitudes to economics and politics.

Our society, and increasingly the whole world, is still under the sway of the Enlightenment project. Bound up with the rise of capitalism, this project embraced the idea of progress as achievable through the advance of natural science and the application of calculative reason. The French and American Revolutions at the end of the eighteenth century were the political expressions of the Enlightenment. Both Liberalism and Marxism are children of the Enlightenment. However much Marxism criticized the extremely jejunely individualistic liberal conception of human nature, it remained as wedded as liberalism to the trinity of science, reason and progress. Marxism is, to quote the French philosopher and political theorist, Simone Weil, 'the highest spiritual expression of bourgeois society'.[2] Economic growth is paramount here and, whether through liberalism's 'trickle-down' effects or capitalism's eventual breakdown and socialism's transformation of society, it is the expansion of the productive forces which will bring about progress. Again to refer to Simone

---

1. For a good discussion of these questions, see M. Rose, *The Post-Modern and the Post-Industrial: A Critical Analysis* (Cambridge: Cambridge University Press, 1991).

2. S. Weil, *Oppression in Liberty* (London: Routledge, 1988), p. 131.

Weil, it is the fond belief that by walking sufficiently far on the ground you will eventually rise up into the air.

The core of the Enlightenment project is an idea of instrumental reason which looks to means and not ends, quantity not quality. More and more areas of society are colonized by concepts such as efficiency, rationalization and accountability. It becomes more and more difficult to contest these concepts which are fast becoming the organizing principles of our society. The insane destruction of the coal industry on the grounds that the pits were 'uneconomic' is only the most striking example of this process. On a more intellectual level, this type of thinking is best exemplified by the principle invented by the Italian political sociologist Vilfredo Pareto and much in vogue in contemporary social science—that a measure is to be approved if at least one person benefits and no one loses. This Pareto principle may seem, like appeals to 'efficiency', to be unexceptionable. But this individual quantitative approach has profoundly conservative implications. It equates a rich person's portion of caviar with a square meal for a poor person, provided they cost the same, and thus precludes even the old utilitarian conclusion that transfers from rich to poor will increase the total sum of welfare. While forbidding any redistribution from rich to poor, it will justify any reform which makes the rich better off while leaving the poor in their existing state. It is a measure of the decline of human values in our society that the main theoretical criterion for any proposed reform is whether or not it is 'Pareto-optimal'.

During the twentieth century, however, the progress of instrumental reason has not gone unchallenged. Two World Wars and the birth out of the second of the nuclear bomb has made the whole idea of scientific progress appear profoundly ambivalent. The development of the Industrial Revolution itself has been called into question over the last twenty-five years by the ecological movement: could not industrial expansion result in the ultimate destruction of the planet as serious as any nuclear explosion? Finally, and most profoundly, many women (and a few men) have begun to wonder whether the whole Enlightenment project does not reflect an overwhelmingly male outlook on the world. Although apparently universal in its appeal, the Enlightenment approach to individuality and reason produced a social world made up in the image of man. It is a sobering thought that such a brilliant political theorist and indefatigable activist as Simone Weil who died in 1943, never enjoyed even the right to vote.

The undermining of the Enlightenment project by the events and movements of the twentieth century has been apparently reinforced by the development of the economy itself. The last twenty years have seen an increasing compression of time and space. Intensification of economic competition has resulted in demand for an ever faster turnover time for capital. Corporative enterprise diversifies its products; production and labour become ever more flexible; deregulation is the order of the day; and decision-making is apparently ever more decentralized. The latter is more apparent than real. For, to take the example of Britain, this process has resulted in authoritarian developments which, in the words of a recent influential commentator, include

> the imposition of central controls upon what were largely autonomous institutions such as the universities; the rejection of consultation with interest groups such as the trade unions; the haughty and dismissive treatment of cause groups and professional bodies; the transfer of many local government functions to centrally appointed 'quangos'; severe controls and restrictions upon elected local bodies themselves; more partisan appointments to official positions; a strong use of the Official Secrets Act to prevent discussion of the behaviour of the state's security forces; the 'doctoring' of official statistics; and an unprecedented extension of the government's public relations machinery to promote its policies and hobble its critics. All this was accompanied by an angry and intolerant attitude towards both opponents and independent critics such as the Church of England and the British Broadcasting Corporation.[3]

The paradox is that the 'free' market results in the centralization of economic and political power: the market is a dictatorship all the more implacable for its being impersonal.

These economic developments have been accompanied by profound cultural changes which are often referred to as postmodernity. They can be summed up in one phrase: the aestheticization of politics. Consider, for example, the fact that an ex-movie actor can be elected and re-elected president of the United States in spite of the majority of the American citizens being opposed to all his major policies. This is indeed the triumph of aesthetics over ethics, of package over content. This process is made possible by the predominance of the fleeting image over a narrative which involves a past and a future, a sense of direction. A perpetual becoming precludes any sense of being.[4]

3. P. Self, *Government by the Market?* (London: Macmillan, 1993), p. 244.
4. See further: D. Harvey, *The Condition of Post-Modernity* (Oxford: Basil Blackwell, 1990), Part III.

All this sounds deeply disconcerting. Yet it should be remembered that the Enlightenment project and the postmodern movement do contain profoundly emancipatory ideas. Can the idea of human rights so central to the former and the uninhibited pluralism of the latter offer us any resources today? With its individualist and anti-clerical origins, the concept of rights is one with which the Christian tradition has found it difficult to come to terms. I tend to agree with the view of Simone Weil that 'the notion of obligation comes before that of rights which are inferior and subordinate to the former'.[5] But the idea of rights is so ingrained in the European tradition of political thought from 1789 onwards that it at least makes sense to ask to build upon it. However understandable the emphasis on political rights may have been in the reconstruction of post-war Europe, with the memory of Hitler and the presence of Stalin, the collapse of Communism and the end of the Cold War afford a welcome opportunity for this generation of rights to be followed by a second generation dealing with the social and economic spheres. The ravages of pure market liberalism recently in both East and West make emphasis on these rights all the more urgent. In their recent pastoral letter the United States Catholic Bishops quoted the statement of John Paul II in 1984 that 'the needs of the poor take priority over the desires of the rich; the rights of workers over the maximization of profit; the production to meet social needs over production for military purposes'.[6] The hierarchy drew the obvious conclusion that

> In order to create a new kind of political democracy the founders of our nation were compelled to develop ways of thinking and political institutions which had never existed before…we believe that the time has come for a similar experiment in economic democracy; the creation of an order that guarantees the minimum conditions of human dignity in the economic sphere for every person.[7]

From a theological point of view, human rights spring from the realization that all people are created in the image of God and therefore have equal human worth. In order to fulfil their vocation as the bearers of God's image, the fundamental rights of all people are to be fully claimed and fully appropriated. It is evident that people are not able to realize

5.   S. Weil, *The Need for Roots* (London: Routledge & Kegan Paul, 1952), p. 3.
6.   *Economic Justice for All: Catholic Social Teaching and the USA* (National Catholic Documentary Service, 1986), para. 94.
7.   Quoted in J. Cort, *Christian Socialism* (Maryknoll, NY: Orbis, 1988), p. 331. This passage was omitted from the final draft.

their potential without certain basic rights. To prevent people from acquiring these rights is to frustrate the work of God in the world. The popular culture of the Christian Church is not accustomed, however, to see this as a violation of human rights. It will require a fundamental change in perception for the average Christian community to see home-lessness and unemployment as the product of destructive and sinful structures which stand in much more urgent need of reform than many other areas which traditionally enjoy a greater prominence in pulpit and pew.

Less consonant, however, with the Enlightenment project and its industrial society is what has been called the third generation of human rights—those of a developmental or ecological nature. Here the Christian religion has at best an ambivalent record: a strong theme in much ecological writing has been the responsibility of the Judaeo-Christian tradition for a good proportion of the destructive attitude to nature that now threatens us all with catastrophe. In 1967 Lynn White published what was to become a much-discussed article entitled 'The Historical Roots of our Ecological Crisis',[8] in which he claimed that by destroying pagan animism Christianity had made it possible to exploit nature in a mood of indifference to any intrinsic value that natural objects might contain and that, therefore, Christianity bore a huge burden of guilt in encouraging the birth of science and technology, the conjunction of which had given to humanity powers that, to judge their ecological effects, were out of control. His conclusion was that 'we shall continue to have a worsening ecologic crisis until we reject the Christian axiom that nature has no reason for existence save to serve man'.[9] Thus White can be seen as extending the link that Weber tried to establish between protestantism and capitalism to that between Christianity and nature as a whole. And perhaps that link should be seen, in White's case as in Weber's, as a functional rather than a directly causal relationship.

It is, of course, also argued that there is present in the Christian tradi-tion a parallel and contrasting view of humanity as the 'steward' of nature in that 'the earth is the Lord's and the fullness thereof'. The idea of stewardship is an unfortunate one here: it implies an absent God and is inherently male since its female counterpart inevitably brings to mind one of the less attractive aspects of modern air travel. Nevertheless, basing themselves on the second account of creation in Genesis many

8. First published in *Science* 155 (March, 1967), pp. 1203-1207.
9. White, 'Our Ecological Crisis', p. 1207.

Christian moralists, theologians and philosophers, from those who rejected the Gnostics' antipathy to nature onwards, have defended the view that people have obligations with respect to many non-humans and that the flourishing of non-humans is of intrinsic value.[10] Whether it is possible to express these concerns in terms of rights is open to doubt.

The best examples of these different traditions with God's creative activity can be found in religious orders such as the Franciscans, the Benedictines and the Cistercians. Probably no other saint in the history of Christianity has been more identified with a reverence for nature than Francis of Assisi—whom White proposes as a patron saint of ecologists. The view that we are but a part of a unitary and all-embracing natural order with which we should try to live in harmony is an abiding tradition in Western thought from Erigena and Duns Scotus through Wordsworth, Shelley, Coleridge and the Romantics to its most striking expression in some of the poetry of Gerard Manley Hopkins. A philosophical counterpart to Hopkins's poetry is to be found in the work of Teilhard de Chardin who set out to formulate an evolutionary metaphysics in which the growing consciousness of humanity would enable it to participate in the self-creation of nature and help it to attain that Omega Point which is its ultimate goal.[11]

The issues raised by the current ecological crisis cannot be accommodated within existing Western political traditions. This is obviously so with the currently dominant market liberalism; since it is difficult to see how any society based on the principles of private enterprise could possibly cope with the colossal contemporary threats to our environment. Almost any other branch of Western political thought—from anarchism on the extreme left, to Fascism on the extreme right—has *some* aspects of green thought.[12]

This is obviously so with anarchism whose principles as expounded by, say, Murray Bookchin, fit well with the typical green espousal of a de-centralized, non-hierarchical participatory society committed to a no-growth economy. Kropotkin and William Morris could be seen as

10. See, for example, M. Grey, *Redeeming the Dream: Feminism, Redemption and the Christian Tradition* (London: SPCK, 1989), ch. 3.

11. For an impressive ecological theology based on Teilhardian principles, see S. McDonagh, *To Care for the Earth: A Call to a New Theology* (London: Chapman, 1986).

12. Cf. P. Hay, 'Ecological Values and Western Political Traditions', *Politics* 8 (October, 1988), pp. 22ff.

worthy forerunners of green politics; and St. Francis himself is a true spiritual democrat some of whose followers—at least as portrayed in *The Name of the Rose*[13]—have distinctly anarchist overtones. The fundamental eco-centrism of green thought does indeed mark it off from other political currents, but it is undoubtedly with some forms of the socialist tradition that it has most in common. I say 'some' here mindful that mainstream Marxism in some of its theory and most of its practice has shared with capitalism the belief that the growth of the productive forces would in some way bring about the salvation of society. Nevertheless, the strong ascetic tradition in Christianity, allied with a socialist idea of pervasive material solidarity, could undoubtedly contribute to dealing with the environmental problems we face.

The task of curbing the imperialism of economic rationality is so daunting that only some kind of strong spiritual base can sustain it. The difficulty is that the impact of postmodern attitudes has been ambivalent: profoundly liberating in some respects (think of the work of Foucault on power), it has, at the same time, undermined the authority of previous 'grand narratives' of history. All that is solid has indeed seemed to melt into air as universal moral principles, rationality and the very notion of the self have appeared to be without foundation. And what use are rights without a self to appropriate them?

Intellectually, this challenge can be met in two broad ways. The first is to stick to the universal moral principles inherent in modernity. On this view, in order to avoid lapsing into cynical relativism, we need defensible ethical foundations. The most influential opponent of this view is the German social philosopher Jürgen Habermas who claims that the very act of speech involves the supposition of the possibility of an ideal speech situation in which the force of the better argument alone will decide the issue. For people speaking to each other aim at reaching some kind of understanding. Communicative interaction, for Habermas, presupposes that those engaging in it could sustain four types of validity claim: first, that what they say is comprehensible; secondly, that it is true; thirdly, that it is legitimate in the context; and lastly, that it is sincerely meant. The redemption of these claims is only possible if all members of society have an equal chance to participate in the discussion; and this involves the notion of the transformation of society in a direction that would enable such a communicative competence to characterize all members of society. For technological society can only be rational if its policies are

13. U. Eco, *The Name of the Rose* (London: Secker & Warburg, 1983).

subject to public control. But, for this to happen, discussion and opinion would have to be free from manipulation and domination. The ultimate goal of social emancipation is, therefore, inherent in any and every speech act,[14] The second approach, best exemplified in the work of Alasdair Macintyre, rejects the universal rational liberalism of the Enlightenment in favour of a more communitarian approach which emphasizes the social embeddedness of our thought. Drawing heavily on Aristotle, Macintyre claims that there is no 'view from nowhere', no rationality independent of particular conceptions of the good life, and no set rules or principles which can claim validity independent of our conception of the good. As opposed to the abstract universal liberal individualism of the Enlightenment, the emphasis here is on the tradition of particular communities in which the virtues are understood in the context of the goals of that community and exemplified in practices through standards of excellence which are internal to that practice.[15]

What both these very different approaches have in common is the attempt to limit the expansive imperialism of industrial society. They are a demand for life and the living environment to be withdrawn from the domination of economics. In the words of André Gorz, 'this boils down to saying that economic activity has meaning only if it serves something other than itself'.[16] For economics is a clear example of 'cognitive-instrumental reasoning': a science for calculating the effectiveness of means, and selecting the most effective means to achieve a given end. It cannot be applied to ends which are not distinct from the means employed, and cannot in itself determine what ends should be pursued. He continues,

> When it is not supplied with an end, it chooses those ends for which it possesses the most effective means: it will adopt as a target the expansion of the sphere in which its own rationality applies, and will tend to subject to this sphere all others, including life and the natural foundations of life. This predominance of economic rationality over all other forms of rationality is the essence of capitalism. Left to itself, it would end by extinguishing all life and would thus itself become extinct.

14. See S.K. White, *Three Recent Work of Jürgen Habermas: Reason, Justice and Modernity* (Cambridge: Cambridge University Press, 1988).

15. See A. Macintyre, *After Virtue* (London: Duckworth, 1981); and the essays collected by S. Mendus and J. Horton (eds.), *After MacIntyre* (Cambridge: Polity Press, 1994).

16. A. Gorz, 'Political Ecology: Expertocracy versus Self-limitation', in *New Left Review* (December 1993).

Increasingly, people are beginning to question the industrial ideology of growth and compensatory consumption which involves ecological destruction and the appalling exploitation of the South by the North. Work-sharing, co-operative enterprises, the uncoupling of income from work-time are all going to be high on the agenda. What we need is less work and less consumption combined with more autonomy and therefore security as to basic income.

The transformation of society here implied may seem unobtainable. But we should bear in mind first that it may well be forced upon us by the sheer unsustainability of economic growth; and secondly, that the desire for ever-increasing consumption is a relatively recent phenomenon: until about 150 years ago the norm was a stable conception of sufficiency to which the idea of working harder to increase one's standard of living was quite alien. Moreover, it is simply not the case that there are no viable alternative ways of organizing our economic system: the difficulty is rather that those who profit most from the present organization of the economy are too powerful and will not permit change.[17] But change will have to come and the values so sterlingly exemplified in the work of South Yorkshire's Industrial Mission should be at its very centre.

17. For a good discussion of alternative way of organizing a viable economic democracy, see D. Schweikart, *Against Capitalism* (Cambridge: Cambridge University Press, 1993).

CHRISTIAN ECONOMIC POLICIES? ETHICAL REFLECTIONS ON BRITISH GOVERNMENTS OVER THREE DECADES

Peter Cope

Introduction

Can the economic policies of any government be properly described as to any degree 'Christian'? This is the question I set out to examine, and so the question-mark in the title is very important!

Some economists, politicians and Christians would strongly deny the possibility of applying the term 'Christian' to economic policies. Economics is a social science, and macro-economics is largely about inflation and unemployment and the determination of the total output of the economy. Most economists who advise politicians try to follow scientific procedures and methods, and thus to exclude particular moral values which they may hold. However, as Andrew Britton has pointed out

> It would be naive to pretend that economics is always objective and scientific in method. Throughout the history of the subject its main purpose has been to guide economic policy, and economists have always been inspired by political visions and ideals as well as the quest for truth.[1]

Politicians in government who implement particular economic policies have—in contrast to economists—to be fairly explicit about their values, but these values must be part of their broad political vision. In 1990s' Britain most leading politicians either do not derive their political inspiration from the Christian faith, or if they do are often cautious about admitting it. The late John Smith was definitely in the second category: he once gave an inspiring address to the Christian Socialist movement, and yet would freely admit that while his own political vision was inspired by his faith, others came to the same conclusions by a different route. Perhaps such an attitude is inevitable for everyone who seeks a

---

1.   A. Britton, 'Is there a Distinctively Christian Approach to Economics?' (Audenshaw Paper [AP147]; Oxford: The Hinksey Centre, 1993).

broad measure of support across a pluralist society.

Christians who would not wish to apply the label 'Christian' to economic policies can be found throughout the churches: after all, sermons or discussions on this topic are still fairly unusual. However, Christians for whom faith is exclusively personal in nature would be more likely to take this line—such as might be found amongst conservative evangelical or fundamentalist groups. For them, individuals are Christian when they accept Jesus as Lord and Saviour; and so it follows that communities and institutions can only be described as 'Christian' when they are largely or entirely composed of individuals who have made that faith commitment. Such people would usually deny the possibility of people living by 'Christian values' without conscious allegiance to Jesus Christ.

So to claim that particular economic policies of government could be described as 'Christian' is fraught with difficulty for people in 1990s' Britain. Maybe this difficulty is a measure of how far Christian thinkers have acquiesced in the privatization of religious faith and its moral implications, and is—for people outside the churches—a cumulative result of generations in which this attitude has been accepted almost unthinkingly.

I want to claim—at least as a working hypothesis—that it is possible to describe some economic policies as 'Christian', but on the important condition that they can be shown to fulfil a number of demonstrably Christian criteria. I use the word 'demonstrably' advisedly. In view of the difficulties already mentioned, the temptation for Christians may be to develop a distinctively Christian approach: in other words, to contrast Christian moral values and their implications with other contemporary moral values. Andrew Britton tries to do this in the paper to which I have already referred, and he criticizes Christians who 'accept the agenda of "political economy" and address the familiar issues of the state versus the market, equality versus efficiency'. He takes three points of New Testament teaching on economics, and develops valuable perspectives from them.

However, Andrew himself admits that his is 'a highly uncomfortable' approach to economics which leaves the task of applying Christian ethics 'difficult, if not impossible'. I would be the last to minimize the difficulties of the Christian ethicist, but it does seem to me that he handicaps himself by a desire to produce distinctive Christian moral reflections, and therefore deliberately takes New Testament perspectives which contrast with contemporary values.

The approach I prefer to take in this paper is to consider both the Old and New Testaments, together with insights from the tradition of Christian teaching since then, and produce twelve demonstrably Christian criteria, moral perspectives, by which to judge economic policies. These may or may not produce conclusions which contrast with contemporary values. However, at least the judgment as to whether they should or should not be included is made on the grounds, not of whether they are distinctively Christian, but whether they are both significant and morally useful within the Judaeo-Christian tradition.

A Method of Making Christian Judgments of Complex Issues

A number of recent writers have produced general statements of moral value derived from the Christian faith, including Philip Wogaman's 'moral presumptions',[2] Donald Hay's 'Biblical principles for economic life',[3] Ronald Preston's 'considerations' suggested by 'a Christian critique of the social order',[4] Brian Griffiths's 'Christian Guidelines for economic life',[5] and John Atherton's 'general considerations of faith'.[6] In developing my method, I am certainly indebted to them for some of what follows. However, I prefer the concept of a Christian moral perspective because it is a view of the world of human experience from a position firmly established within the Christian faith and tradition.

You will appreciate that because of the constraints of space, it is only possible to give a very brief description of my ethical method. My purpose is to give you at least an outline of how I derive my conclusions, but it is the conclusions themselves that I want to share in some detail. For those particularly interested in this method, I have simplified and adapted it for general use by Christians for making many different Christian moral decisions.[7]

2. P. Wogamon, *A Christian Method of Moral Judgement* (London: SCM Press, 1976).

3. D. Hay, *Economics Today: A Christian Critique* (Leicester: Apollos, 1989), pp. 70ff.

4. R. Preston, *Religion and the Persistence of Capitalism* (London: SCM Press, 1979), p. 48

5. B. Griffiths, *Morality and the Market Place* (London: Hodder & Stoughton, 1982), pp. 91ff.

6. J. Atherton, *Faith in the Nation* (London: SPCK, 1988), p. 142.

7. P. Cope, 'The Incredible Flying Machine: A Way of Making Christian Decisions' (unpublished paper, available from the author).

The method which I developed in my thesis[8] has a number of different stages:

1. *Deriving a major issue to be examined.* In my thesis I examined two themes, one of which was the management of the British economy (1965-85), and I formulated the following issue to be examined:

> What should be the priorities of an advanced economy in Britain, with particular reference to the levels of inflation and unemployment?

2. *Examining this issue through 12 Christian moral perspectives.* These complement each other in order to produce specific implications for the issue. The perspectives are as follows (unfortunately space does not allow me to describe them):

> P.1: Physical existence as created and redeemed by God, and therefore good.
> P.2: The value and dignity of each human life.
> P.3: The unity of the human family in God.
> P.4: The equal worth of all persons in God.
> P.5: Human responsibility to steward God's creation, and to promote love and justice.
> P.6: Human freedom as God-given.
> P.7: Human vocation as God-given.
> P.8: The priority of grace over works in the treatment of people.
> P.9: Priority for the Poor.
> P.10: The State as God-given.
> P.11: Human finitude and limitations.
> P.12: Human sinfulness.

3. *Drawing together the implications for the issue from each of the 12 perspectives to form a Specific Moral Objective (SMO).* An SMO represents a possible and provisional statement of how the Christian faith can bear on a particular area of public policy. It must be faithful to the major outcome from each perspective, even when they appear to lead in different directions, and therefore often represents something of a compromise. Some people may find this irritating or frustrating, but the reality is that the moral values of the Christian faith, when taken in their entirety, often lead to conflicting conclusions in complex situations in social ethics. The only way compromise can be avoided is to omit some

---

8.   P. Cope, 'A Theological Exploration of the Changing Role of Government in the Economy with Particular Reference to Industrial Relations in Britain, 1965–85' (PhD thesis, Manchester University, 1991).

values altogether, but the price of more clear-cut judgments is to do less than justice to the comprehensiveness of the Christian revelation.

After following through the method, the SMO which I formulated for the issue above was:

> A government should have as its economic priority the greatest possible level of employment consonant with an inflation level of no more than (say) 5%. To this end, government should seek to expand the economy at a sustainable rate (perhaps $2\frac{1}{2}\%$ per annum), ensuring environmentally-friendly policies wherever possible. (A further priority should be investment to improve the minimum standards of income, health, housing and education. The more efficient use of existing resources, the promotion of greater producer competition, and better re-training and re-location provisions are further and subsidiary objectives.)

Unfortunately the amount of statistical monitoring of welfare benefits and standards in housing, health care and education required to test the above priority was quite beyond the scope of my thesis, and so had to be excluded from the study. The same applies to the subsequent priority on the use of resources, the promotion of competition and re-training and re-location provisions. Hence the brackets around these sentences.

4. *The interactive element.* This recognizes that moral thinking must be a two-way process, rather than merely an application of Christian values to a secular issue. On the one hand, the themes have been reflected on through 12 Christian moral perspectives to produce an SMO, which represents a possible Christian benchmark for economic policy. On the other, the results of these reflections themselves raise questions for the overall understanding of the perspectives. Unfortunately, there is no space to go into further detail here.

5. *Using the SMO above as a possible yet provisional Christian standard by which to appraise the performance of different British governments in the years 1965–85* (See Section 3).

Appraising the Economic Priorities of British Government 1965–85

October 1964–May 1970 Labour (Harold Wilson)
This government operated in an economic context in which unemployment could scarcely have been called a problem by the standards of recent years. For the whole of this period unemployment remained at

below 3%, as Britain shared in the post-war manufacturing boom with many other countries. At the same time it was recognized that to maintain current prosperity, and to keep inflation under control, productivity would have to be improved, and wages limited to this rate of growth. Hence the famous national plan of prices, productivity and incomes of 1965, which was meant to commit employers and trades unions to this goal. In practice this national plan was completely ineffective, and deflationary packages had to be introduced in 1966 and 1967, including a period of statutory and voluntary incomes policies.

In the light of the SMO, a Christian judgment might be that this government attempted to maintain a high level of employment and a low level of inflation, although the effects of its strategy on inflation were not successful; wage inflation in 1964 was 4%, but had risen to 10% by 1970. Economic growth up to 1965 was averaging 3% annually, but slowed to an average of 2.4% for the rest of the period. However, the fact that such relatively healthy growth was maintained must be seen more as a continuation of the post-war boom than the result of deliberate government policy. In fact, government contribution to growth in terms of efforts to encourage increased productivity largely failed.

June 1970–February 1974 Conservative (Edward Heath)

Following the failure of the previous government to control wage inflation, Heath encouraged policies for industrial expansion as a way of absorbing this and restoring British competitiveness. It was described as the 'dash for growth', with taxation reduced to restore some incentives for investment. In fact, the climate was scarcely appropriate for such growth. The Industrial Relations Act (1971) provoked a very hostile trades union reaction, and related to this were the two miners' strikes of 1972 and 1974. In these circumstances, the average growth figure for these years of 2.25% is remarkable.

However, the wage inflation which this government inherited at about 10% continued to increase, and by November 1972 a statutory incomes policy was introduced to tackle it. While this had a slight effect, by the end of this government's term of office the figure had risen to about 15%. Unemployment still looked relatively favourable, beginning and ending this period at less than 3%, although rising to about 3.5% in 1972.

In terms of the SMO, a Christian judgment might be that in spite of efforts to reduce the rate of inflation, this proved remarkably recalcitrant, and the already too high figure worsened considerably. Yet unemployment continued to be relatively low, and the growth rate reasonable in the circumstances.

March 1974–March 1976 Labour (Harold Wilson)

This government came to power during the second miners' strike (1973-74), and immediately set about negotiating a 'social contract' with the trades unions. This comprised an undertaking by the government to control basic prices, and to introduce a number of important pieces of legislation covering individual and collective employment rights. It also provided for an undertaking by the trades unions to restrain wage increases. This bargain was disastrous in terms of wage inflation, which increased from 15% to nearly 30% within 12 months. That rise provoked a massive crisis of confidence by holders of assets in sterling which eventually led to Wilson's resignation. Besides an ineffective strategy in relation to inflation, this government's record on the other two key indicators was scarcely more promising. Unemployment increased from less than 3% to 5% by the end of 1976, and growth in the economy was virtually nil. This period was described as 'stagflation' by some economists, and represents the end of attempts at Keynesian demand-management of the economy. Injecting further demand into the economy by public spending resulted in both higher prices and, eventually, higher unemployment.

In terms of this SMO, a Christian judgment might be that the economic strategy of this government was completely ineffective at maximizing possible employment, at reducing and restricting the level of inflation, and at maintaining a sustainable level of economic growth.

April 1976–May 1979 Labour (James Callaghan)

In reaction to the international sterling crisis, severe public expenditure cuts were announced by government. When this was not sufficient to restore confidence, a large loan package was agreed with the International Monetary Fund in December 1976, the price of which was further cuts in government spending. The particular achievement of this government was to negotiate an effective incomes policy with the trades union movement which lasted for three years, reducing wage inflation to 15% in 1976 and 5% in 1977. Unfortunately this created pressures for wage rises in the public sector which led to the 'winter of discontent' (1978–79), to another sharp rise in wage inflation (15% at end of 1979), and to the eventual defeat of the government. Unemployment rose slightly, but at the end of the period was only about 5.5%. Economic growth throughout this period was remarkably good, averaging at 3.2% for the years 1976–79, reflecting the benefit of controlling the rise in incomes.

Making a Christian judgment on this government in the light of the SMO, it can be said that the anti-inflation strategy was successful—at least, over a period of two years; although (like most other experiments in incomes policy) it simply restrained wage inflation and in so doing produced an even larger explosion in the long run. On the other hand, the rate of economic growth was remarkably good, and the rate of unemployment remained under control, if still too high.

June 1979–(1985)[9] Conservative (Margaret Thatcher)
This government inherited relatively high wage and price inflation which was further increased by a sharp rise in Value Added Tax. In 1980 the figure reached about 17%, but then began to fall steadily as the government's tight restrictions on public spending and on the money supply began to take effect. The unprecedented speed of the rise in the level of unemployment also had an effect on wage negotiations. Hence from 1982 inflation was below 6%, which is a remarkable achievement in view of Britain's performance over the previous ten years. However, the public spending and money supply measures largely responsible for this helped to generate massive unemployment: the level rose from about 5.5% in 1979 to 13.5% in 1985, which represented over 3.3 million people. Over one million people in 1985 had been unemployed for more than one year. In terms of economic growth, the first three years of this government were very unsuccessful: the economy did not grow at all between 1979 and 1982, but actually contracted by 2.8% during those years. This reflects the considerable number of manufacturing companies which collapsed during the period, with serious consequences for employment. However, in the next three years (1982–85) the economy grew very successfully—by an average of 3.5% per year.

In fairness it should be acknowledged that after 1985, as this government continued in office, the performance of the indicators of unemployment and inflation changed significantly: after reaching a peak in 1985, the level of unemployment gradually fell to just over 1.6 million at the end of 1989, whereas the rate of inflation slowly rose to 7.8% by the same date.

9. 1985 appears here because my paper examines the changing role of government in the economy in Britain between 1965 and 1985.

Using the SMO to make a Christian judgment, it might be said that this government was clearly more successful than any of its predecessors in reducing inflation to something approaching the level of Britain's international competitors (although the slow rise after 1986 demonstrates that the phenomenon is still not under control). After a very difficult start, it also produced conditions to encourage a substantial and sustained rate of economic growth.

However, the market-based philosophy which produced this real success also led to a different governmental attitude to unemployment. Instead of the interventionist demand-management policies of most of its predecessors to reduce unemployment, this government allowed the level of unemployment to rise steeply and concentrated on strengthening the supply side in terms of enterprise incentives and skills training, together with legislation to free the labour market by curbing union activity. While it may be recognized that much unemployment in the period was caused by lack of competitiveness and inefficiency in British industry, it must also be said that this government's refusal to adopt the suggestions of many commentators[10] and implement selective projects of public investment in Britain's decaying infrastructure led to considerably higher unemployment than would otherwise have been the case.

Section 4: Epilogue

I hope I have shown that it is possible to use values based on the Bible and Christian tradition to produce a provisional standard or benchmark by which the macro-economic policies of different governments can be judged. Because of limitations of space, I cannot include in the paper a detailed description of the Christian moral perspectives, nor the large amount of reflections from the perspectives which produced the SMO. The SMO may therefore appear quite arbitrary. If you want to check this method in detail, I suggest you consult my original thesis,[11] or if this proves impractical the simplified version I wrote up in 'The Incredible Flying Machine'.[12]

10. For example, A. Storkey, *Transforming Economics* (London: SPCK, 1986); R. Layard, *How to Beat Unemployment* (Oxford: Oxford University Press, 1986); D. Steel, 'A Ten Point Strategy', quoted in D. Coates and J. Hilliard, *The Economic Revival of Modern Britain* (Aldershot: Edward Elgar, 1987).
11. Cope, 'Changing Role of Government'.
12. Cope, 'Incredible Flying Machine'.

One important further point I would like to make is this. The SMO which appears on p. 84 was produced by reflecting on the theme (also on p. 84) in the light of the macro-economic policies and experience of British governments between 1965 and 1985. It follows that as these policies and experience changed in later years, so the SMO needs to change as well.

In October 1990 official unemployment stood at 1.67 million, and it was clear that the British economy was in recession. After the Lawson £4 billion tax-cutting budget of March 1988, wage and price inflation was fuelled until it had reached 10.9% by November 1990, in spite of maintaining interest rates at 15% for a considerable time. It was clear that the sales of—and therefore the jobs in—British companies would be badly affected unless inflation could be reduced. Other relevant factors were the shrinking of the defence industry, and the increasing awareness of potential environmental damage.

I therefore suggested the following SMO for the British economy at the end of 1990:

> In order to safeguard the prospects for employment in Britain, government should take all possible steps to reduce current inflation to 5% or less. A further priority should be investment to improve minimum standards of income, health, housing and education. The costs of necessary environmental improvement should be met and equitably shared between government and consumers. The more efficient use of existing resources, the promotion of greater producer competition, and better re-training and re-location provisions are further objectives.

Three and a half years later, the major indicators have changed again. Inflation is now 2.6% (July 1994), and official unemployment figures have been improving—but only very slowly (July 1994, unemployment = 2.64 million). Britain continues to be affected by the persistent recession in Europe, which is increasingly threatened in manufacturing industries by the low cost base of the Pacific Rim countries including China.

An SMO now would certainly have to address the issue of excessively high unemployment in Britain—as in most of the rest of the European Union—and the urgent need for new measures to reduce it significantly. One possible solution creates a difficult ethical dilemma: some economists have suggested that the only way to reconcile the present market system with the need to generate far more jobs is to create these jobs at very low wage levels. Yet what of the need for rewards which are seen to be fair, and of the need for a more egalitarian society? For Christians, good economic policies will always need a sound basis in justice if they are to be acceptable.

A JUST AND FRUITFUL CREATION

Anne Primavesi

At the time of the political gathering of the United Nations Conference on Environment and Development (UNCED) at Rio in 1992, the World Council of Churches (WCC) held a parallel conference there in one of the poorest and most deprived suburbs. This conference was entitled 'Searching for the New Heavens and the New Earth: A Christian Response to the United Nations Conference'. At the very first session, a queue rapidly formed at the microphone to challenge the title on the grounds that it was not an accurate translation of the text from the Apocalypse. The text reads,

> And I saw a new heaven and a new earth, for the first heaven and the first earth had passed away. (Rev. 21.1)

This was being taken as the fulfilment of the promise recorded in Isaiah, the promise of a new creation:

> For behold, I create new heavens and a new earth (Isa. 65.17); the new heavens and the new earth which I will make shall remain before me. (Isa. 66.22)

One of those who queued, a scientist, objected to the title itself. He evoked some laughter when he said indignantly, 'We don't need a new earth. What we need is a clean earth!'

Echoing this protest from Rio, I want to say: We don't need a new creation. What we need is a just creation! In Isaiah, the protest against injustice, in the context of the new creation, takes many forms. Following on the passage quoted, it is specifically against the fact that those who build houses do not inhabit them; that those who plant vineyards do not eat their fruits. This is the image I shall use to discuss issues of justice in North–South relations, taking it to represent both those who plant and those who eat the fruits. The terms 'North' and 'South' remain broadly synonymous with 'rich' and 'poor', 'developed' and 'developing' nations, although neither is a uniform or permanent grouping, or wholly satisfactory to those designated by either term. We have, for instance, in this country as in the United States, the 'South' in the North, those poor whose standard of living has fallen in real terms over the past twelve years to well below the 'poverty line'.

I shall use the image of planting and eating fruits within the context of one of the themes of this conference: the economy. In particular, I set it within the framework of IMSY's Mission Statement, which affirms that social and economic structures are means through which people share in God's purpose that creation be fruitful and harmonious, and that those structures which destroy the integrity of creation, and which oppress people in body, mind or spirit, run counter to God's purpose and must be opposed.

The global economy dominated by the concept of free markets affects the lives not only of those who plant the fruit and cannot eat it, but of those who do eat it, the consumers. We who live in the Northern consumerist society are increasingly aware of the injustice of an economic system which forces the producer to grow and to sell fruit which the producer cannot afford either to eat or to sell. While this may always have been the case (not many market garden workers eat asparagus), now it is the scale of production and consumption and the inbuilt injustice of the system as a whole which causes concern to some Christians today. The number concerned remains low as long as the system is rationalized through the spurious image of a level playing field: as one of equal rights to buy or to sell.

Over fifty years ago, Simone Weil exposed its spuriousness in a vivid metaphor. If, she said, someone tries to brow-beat a farmer to sell his eggs at a moderate price, the farmer can say: 'I have the right to keep my eggs if I don't get a good enough price'. But if a young girl is being forced into a brothel she cannot talk about her rights. In such a situation the word would sound ludicrously inadequate.[1]

Thirty years after Weil, Dorothee Sölle had such a ludicrously inadequate response from Rudolf Bultmann. Taking her example of banana growers exploited by the United Fruit company, he said: 'If the latter does not pay the banana grower enough, he could always take them to

---

1. S. Weil, 'On Human Personality', Appendix in D. McLellan, *Utopian Pessimist: The Life and Thought of Simone Weil* (New York: Poseidon Press, 1990), p. 280.

court or go on strike.'[2] Sölle said: 'I had to laugh at that, but also weep.'[3] I also want to weep: to weep in company with the women who heard Jesus say: 'If this is done in the green wood, what shall be done in the dry?' This theological blindness is symptomatic of what Sölle calls apartheid theology. Apartheid is not merely a political system: it is a particular way of thinking, feeling and living without consciousness of what is going on all around us. It is a way of doing theology without ever letting the poor and economically exploited become visible or audible.[4]

Those aware of what is going on know that the Southern farmer cannot in fact invoke her right to a fair price and take her produce home if the price does not come up to her expectations. She is forced to grow and to sell her produce for a price decided on by the buyer. Increasingly, this buyer acts directly for or on behalf of some Northern importer. Cash-cropping, as this practice is known, is imposed on her by a government desperate to get hard currency to repay its debts to Northern financial institutions. In July 1994 Christian Aid launched a 'Who Runs the World?' campaign to highlight the effects of World Bank and IMF policies. National governments have these policies imposed on them as part of structural adjustment programmes aimed at debt repayment.[5] They force the farmer to grow crops for export rather than staple food for her family to eat. I say *her* family, for worldwide, women produce— and I mean dig and sow and reap and harvest—more than 50% of food; in Africa it is 80%.[6]

What is justice here? The relationship between producer and consumer is a complex one, its mechanisms hidden for the most part by the markets which control it. Taking it at its simplest, the struggle for justice in this relationship is the struggle to minimize harm to both parties. This may seem a very minimalist claim indeed. It does, however, correspond to Simone Weil's definition of justice: *Justice consists in seeing that no harm is done to anyone.*[7] At the very least, it would generally be agreed that, in a just and fruitful creation, producer and consumer should suffer

2.   Quoted in D. Sölle, *The Window of Vulnerability: A Political Spirituality* (Philadelphia: Fortress Press, 1990), p. 128.

3.   Sölle, *Window of Vulnerability*.

4.   Sölle, *Window of Vulnerability*.

5.   See J. Madeley, D. Sullivan and J. Woodroffe, *Who Runs the World?* (London: Christian Aid, 1994), pp. 22-60.

6.   Official Report, World Women's Congress for a Healthy Planet (New York: WEDO, 1992), p. 19.

7.   Weil, *Human Personality*, p. 286.

no obvious harm from their relationship. We, in the consumerist culture of the economic North, have safeguarded ourselves in various ways from harm; EU directives and consumer associations are set up for this purpose. The Rio process (by which I mean the preparatory commissions, the conference itself, the documents issuing from the process and the various non-governmental and other organizations pledged to carry on the process and implement agreed policies) is pledged to protect the poor producer by improving the sustainability of natural resources in the economic South. The European Ecumenical Organisation for Development, for instance, calls for credit and subsidies to promote peasant and family farming and to market diversified crops.

However, such generalized expressions of benevolence cease to have much meaning in the light of World Bank and IMF structural adjustment policies. They have ceased to have much meaning for me personally since, at the Rio conference, I was forced to consider the North as producer and the South as consumer, consumer of the deadly fruits of Northern industries. Accustomed as we are to see the exotic fruits of Southern labour imported for our nourishment, we seldom think of the lethal fruits we export for the consumption of the South. Isaiah's image, as I read it, places an obligation on the producer also: to taste the fruit produced to ensure that it will not harm the consumer. In respect to the North, that obligation, to my knowledge, has never been properly acknowledged either in law or in practice, and seldom in preaching or in theological exposition of belief. I am speaking, of course, of the deadly fruits of the arms trade.

Simone Weil goes on from her general statement that 'Justice consists in seeing that no harm is done to anyone' to express vividly the actual experience of injustice. Whenever, she says, anyone cries inwardly: 'Why am I being hurt?' harm is being done to that person. He or she may often be mistaken when they try to define the harm, and why and by whom it is being inflicted. But the cry itself is infallible.[8]

I heard that cry at Rio. The WCC invited me to their conference to speak on militarism. The subject had been banned from the political agenda by the United States with Britain's support, so the Brazilian bishops asked the WCC specifically to address it. Two-thirds of the audience, again by a conscious decision, was made up of representatives from the South. Their presence was a reminder and a confession of injustice, the injustice done to them by the North in depriving them of

8.   Weil, *Human Personality*.

the power to implement the changes necessary for them to have sustainable economies.

Some of the reasons for the maintenance of this injustice, as seen by those afflicted by it, are laid out in a report from the Southern Networks on Environmental Development (African Region). They say, 'The root causes of the environment and development crisis are embedded in the history, structure, systems, technology and above all consciousness, thinking and decision-making processes that underlie northern civilisation'. There is a major element in this history, structure, systems, technology and consciousness which can be summed up in J.S. Mill's words as the *rule of the strongest*.[9] This is the rule of the North. It has been and still is upheld through economic militarism.

I define this economic militarism as: *the rule of the economically strongest through arms production systems and intermediary physical forces. The latter are equipped through massive indebtedness which inescapably binds the countries of the South to economic and environmental slavery*. The economically strongest, the countries of the North, rule indirectly through the armies of Southern military regimes and those kept in power by the military. We need only think of the weapons sanctions wielded against certain groups and not others in recent years to see how this indirect rule functions. Those armies who are equipped incur massive debts, and those debts are serviced by the forced production of cash-crops which are sold either directly to the North or through brokers who provide the foreign currency needed to pay interest on the debts incurred. It is largely these debts which are the target of structural adjustment programmes. The environmental effects of monoculture cash-cropping are dealt with by taking over more and more land and overcropping it, or by buying fertilisers from the transnational corporations of the North and incurring more debt. So, those who plant vineyards in the South cannot eat their fruits. They end up on tables in the North. The fruits of our industry end up as a deadly harvest in the killing fields of the South.

The anti-personnel (AP) landmines in these fields are a paradigm case of the lethal fruits exported from North to South. Any talk of subsidizing sustainable development, in the South or in the North, becomes a propaganda exercise when, as Oxfam states unequivocally, these mines are causing a humanitarian and environmental disaster of massive pro-

9.   J.S. Mill and H. Taylor Mill, *Essays on Sex Equality* (ed. A. Rossi; Chicago: University of Chicago Press, 1970), pp. 131-35.

portions. They litter the globe, with somewhere between 65 to 110 million of them contaminating over 60 countries, (2 million in Bosnia, Herzegovina and Croatia) causing death, mutilation, fear and agricultural and economic paralysis in some of the poorest countries. In many areas, they are scattered randomly on fertile agricultural and pasture land with little tactical use.[10] They cannot distinguish between the footfall of a soldier and that of a child. The cost of each may be only a few US$ on the open market, yet the UN estimates the cost of mine clearance as between US$300 and US$1000 per mine. This is because manufacturers have invested large sums in research which makes the mines more destructive and less detectable, sums not matched by investment into mine-clearance technology. Because legislation is virtually unenforceable in the anarchic conditions of modern guerrilla and counter-insurgency conflicts, civilians will only be protected when the production, transfer and use of AP-mines is totally banned, or at the very least, says Oxfam, their export. In regard to what I have said already about legislation to minimize harm from what we produce, Oxfam calls on the UK to do what it has not done, and ratify the UN Convention on Inhumane Weapons.

In the report *World Military and Social Expenditures*, 1991, there is a special section on the environment. Before I went to Rio I studied these expenditure graphs. I read about the development of nuclear weapons, the implications of committing long-term government funding to the development of Tactical Air to Surface Missiles and other generations of sophisticated technologies occupying research and development departments. Worldwide, in 1991, 47% of government research funding went to military research and development, 1% to environment.[11] Since the end of the Cold War, this military funding has not decreased. In 1992 it still topped US$ 815 billion, equal to the total income of the poorer half of the world's population. Is this the economic graph of a just and fruitful creation?

There are records available in the North of the environmental devastation caused by military installations, such as the chemicals left at the Rocky Mountain Arsenal and the irradiated islands of the South Pacific. There are pictures of flooded valleys, burnt forests, scorched lands and wrecked harbours left by fighting in Cambodia, Afghanistan and East Timor. There are photographs from Africa of endless files of women

10. Oxfam Briefing (Oxford: Oxfam, Feb. 1994), p. 2.
11. R. Sivard, *World Military and Social Expenditures, 1991* (Washington, DC: World Priorities Inc., 1991).

and children in flight from battle fields, ten-year-old boys carrying rifles and little girls dying from shrapnel wounds. In the past few months we have seen pictures of refugees dying of starvation, disease and psychic terror by the roadsides in Rwanda while the roads are patrolled by truckloads of well-fed, heavily armed soldiers. Is this the picture of a just and fruitful creation?

In Rio, the representatives of the South, and of the South in the North, were not interested in the philosophy of violence, its causes and its possible cures. They were not prepared to analyse the economics of the arms trade which is keeping them, as they themselves put it, in economic slavery to the North. They were not concerned with comparing one graph with another to see who invested the most in their destruction: with deciding whether it was Germany, France, China, Russia, the USA or Britain (together responsible for 85% of world arms sales) which had sold arms to their countries. They saw not numbers, not pictures, but their own and others' lives destroyed by these graphs of expenditure, of debt burden, of investment in tanks, land mines, guns, long and short range missiles and ammunition. Their overriding question could not be answered by more information. They asked: Why are we being hurt? Is anyone in the North doing anything about this injustice?

Their question was addressed to theologians as well as to governments. It is addressed to those working in Industrial Mission for the next fifty years. How can our theological resources be used to do something about this massive injustice? As theological work on the doctrine of creation becomes increasingly sophisticated and abstract, are the writers responding more and more to one another, and less and less to the real problems of living justly within creation? What *do* we mean by a just and fruitful creation?

Going back to the Isaiah text, the producers of the South are outraged not only because they cannot eat their own produce but because *we do not*. They are forced to eat what we produce. They have to consume the products of our arms industries while they cannot eat the fruit of their vineyards. They cannot eat their own fruit because they are forced to pay for and to eat ours. The arms industries in the North export the bulk of their deadly produce. Britain is the sixth largest exporter of military equipment in the world. In 1992, Britain exported £1.5 billion of military equipment. In 1993, orders totalled £6 billion. More than three-quarters of sales are to Third World countries. The mines made in Britain are sown not in England's green and pleasant fields, but in the arid ones of

Somalia, Iraqi Kurdistan, Mozambique and Afghanistan.[12] Their people are forced to eat the deadly fruits of our industry.

The arms technologies of today produce sophisticated, highly expensive weapons. So they are not in the hands of the poor, but in the hands of the rich. These include those in the North rich enough to spend vast sums on research and development of yet more deadly weapons as well as those at the centre of power in the South who are rich enough to buy them and rich enough to feed armies strong enough to use them. The well-fed soldiers in Somalia, in Mozambique, in Haiti and Rwanda can carry and brandish their weapons in the faces of the weak and starving.

Billions are spent by the rich on arms for supposed security. How many times will we have to be able to destroy humankind in order to feel secure? And whose security are we talking about? The security of the hungry, the poor? No. We are talking about the security of the well-fed, the educated, those in the North who can build houses and live in them; who can plant vineyards and eat of their fruits. We say we have not enough to give a kilo of bread or rice to each person in the world, but we, the rich, have enough to put aside 20,000 kilos of explosive for every single person. By the year 2000, the plutonium available will be the equivalent of a million atomic bombs.

Where does Christianity in the North place its security? In banks, tanks and bombs? How does it safeguard the prophetic vision of a just and fruitful creation? Shall we continue to justify our export of deadly fruits to be eaten by the poor? From the moment that Christianity became the official religion of the Roman Empire, its history has been marked and marred by militarism, legitimated in the name of the one Christians claim as their messiah. From the moment when Constantine had his infamous dream, the messianic dream articulated by the prophet Isaiah and proclaimed by Jesus at the beginning of his public life faded into the background. His vision of himself as a Spirit-filled messiah who would free slaves and not bind them, who would heal wounds and not inflict them, was obliterated by Christians who slew captives and enslaved and decimated indigenous peoples in his name.

The early onset of this obliteration is evident in the contemporary description by Eusebius of the imperial banquet celebrating the conclusion of the fourth-century Council of Nicea:

12. L. Doyle, reporting in *The Independent*, 6 June 1994, p. 10.

Detachments of the body-guard and troops surrounded the entrance of the palace with drawn swords, and through the midst of them the men of God proceeded without fear into the innermost of the Imperial apartments, in which some were the Emperor's companions at table, while others reclined on couches arranged on either side. One might have thought that a picture of Christ's kingdom was thus shadowed forth.[13]

Who, other than a militarist Christian, could have thought that this was a picture of Christ's kingdom, of the messianic banquet foreshadowed in Jesus's commensality with the poor, the outcast, the sinner? It is clear that the image of a military messiah, protected by soldiers with drawn weapons, with no woman in sight, enabled future generations to proceed 'without fear' in the exercise of that kind of power. The spread of this messiah's kingdom, especially in those countries designated the South, is catalogued by Christine Gudorf:

Christian faith has been used to legitimate the torture and killing of millions in the Crusades, the conquest of the Americas, the Inquisition, and the pogroms which preceded the modern Holocaust. Killing, slavery and torture supposedly legitimised by the gospel have continued in our world, for example in the justification of apartheid in the Dutch Reformed Church of South Africa, or the use of torture and assassination against supposed 'godless Communists' by military regimes which call themselves Christian. But there are, of course, also other, more subtle, though no less real or painful, forms of victimisation in our world for which those who claim the gospel must take responsibility.[14]

Yet Christianity takes as the supreme incarnation and revelation of God a man who taught love of enemies, forgiveness and non-retaliation, who was renowned for healing bodies and attending to their needs, and who died on a cross erected by military power, his body pierced and broken after death by military weapons. There is good reason to believe that many persons in the early centuries of Christianity had their religious sensibilities shaped by this new notion of divine power as healing, suffering and empowering love, and that this image of divinity, rather than coercive omnipotence, evoked their religious worship. They believed that God's agent of deliverance from evil was one who had been the victim, rather than the representative of the coercive powers of this world.

13. Quoted in J.D. Crossan, *The Historical Jesus: The Life of a Mediterranean Jewish Peasant* (San Francisco: Harper San Francisco, 1991), p. 424.
14. C. Gudorf, *Victimization* (Philadelphia: Trinity Press International, 1992), p. 2.

This side of Christian teaching and imagery has continued to influence the sensibilities and lives of certain Christians open to its influence, notably the Quakers and Mennonites. If we do not carry over that prophetic memory of a messianic body which inflicted no wound but suffered many, we have two mutually exclusive images of the messiah, and cannot live credibly with both. Those outside Christianity see this clearly, as do poor Christians living in the South who cry out in protest against the scandal of a Eurocentric Christianity which claims that Jesus was the prophetic messiah. If the claim were valid, Christianity should have changed the world to a non-violent, non-coercive, just and peaceful place. But it hasn't. So we cannot claim that *that* messiah has come.

But the warrior-king messiah, *that* messiah seems to have come already. Yet he bears no relationship to what we know of Jesus, to a type of power compatible with working for a just and fruitful creation. This confusion about the power of God manifested in Jesus has allowed Christians to claim that the messiah has come while living as though he had not.

We need therefore to have the courage to say, with our Jewish brothers and sisters, that the prophetic messiah has not come for us, that justice and peace have not yet been seen to embrace on the earth. We need to say that even the *memory* of the messiah who came to heal the victims of violence has (almost) been lost.

For the memory of that messiah lives in the cry from within creation of those who suffer violence and injustice. I heard that cry in Rio. I heard it again two weeks ago from women in central Europe who have taken it up from a group of modern daughters of Jerusalem. They first stood in one of the city squares in 1987, every Friday between 1:00 and 2:00 p.m., at the start of the Palestinian Intifada, in silent protest against the occupation. The movement spread throughout Israel, with some groups being joined by Arab women. It has spread to other countries, to Serbian 'Women in Black' who, every Wednesday since October 1991, stand in downtown Belgrade in silent protest against the war in Bosnia.

They told us that they wear black to mourn, with the daughters of Jerusalem, for all known and unknown victims of this and all other military regimes—for the destroyed cities, the ethnic cleansing, the raped women, the abandoned children. They wear black as an expression of their resistance to war, as an expression of their refusal to be hostages of a militaristic regime. They are silent because words cannot express such tragedy; because words are used to incite hatred; because the lives of

Serbia's citizens are marked by silence through the regime-controlled media. The women's silence is visible. It is their invitation to everyone to think about themselves and about those whose lives and homes are being destroyed; about the silent dead, about abducted, missing and imprisoned persons. Their visible, persistent, non-violent protest is their way of telling a regime which has arrogated the right to speak on their behalf: Don't speak in our name. We shall do that!

If we do not stand with the Women in Black, with the daughters of Jerusalem, will the mountains fall on us? Will the hills cover us? If we do not speak, will the stones cry out? If we do not speak and act, how will the aim of the Mission Statement be accomplished? It affirms that social and economic structures 'can and will be transformed, enabling all people to fulfil their potential as human beings, through relationships that reflect the Gospel values of love, justice and peace'.[15]

---

15. IMSY Mission Statement, reprinted in P. Bagshaw, *The Church beyond the Church* (Sheffield: IMSY, 1994), pp. 128-29.

TRANSFORMING SPEECH

Peter Selby

The Church's apparent cautious moderation, and its commitment to putting down markers and pragmatic incrementalism, have many advantages and much appeal. Yet these characteristics of social witness lend credence to the complaint of the Christian radicals regarding its shallowness. Recent leadership appears to have preferred that its pronouncements should not be directed towards the elaboration of a fundamental vision of the Good Society, or the theological rationale therefor. Instead it has opted for a reiteration of rather familiar theological norms on the apparent assumption that its audience will accept these familiar verities without much debate, and it has assumed the desirability of a mixed economy welfare state as either good or (for the nonce) inevitable and therefore given. Judging from the writings and the interviews which form the basis for this study, the leaders are confident that they can rely on an already existing consensus on the nature of a healthy commonwealth.[1]

There is a long and distinguished history of what is now Industrial Mission in South Yorkshire, and it is important to acknowledge some of the cost that was borne by many people in the course of that history. There were of course the famous episodes of polarization, but there were other lesser, and less well recorded, ones. There are people who have carried a great deal of the price that has to be paid for involvement in new and pioneering ventures. That is not to embark on a rehearsal of the issues, or to allocate blame; it is simply to say that if you do something new there will be hurt from time to time, and IMSY is indebted to those, most recently Paul Bagshaw, who have chronicled its story and thereby ensured that it is not forgotten.[2] So for the achievement—and the cost—grateful thanks.

So much of what Industrial Mission is about, and indeed so much of

1. H. Clark, *The Church under Thatcher* (London: SPCK, 1993), p. 120.
2. P. Bagshaw, *The Church beyond the Church: Sheffield Industrial Mission 1944–1994* (Sheffield: IMSY, 1994).

the churches' engagement with social and economic issues, has its origin in the pioneering work done here over fifty years. Not just in Britain but among Christians all over the world engaged in social and economic discipleship, Sheffield represents the recognized source of a great deal of good Christian missionary endeavour. And so this seems an appropriate occasion to reflect on what Christian social engagement might mean today.

This is rather a sobering time at which to engage in that kind of thankful reflection. I do not just mean that the churches are not finding it easy, or at least are not choosing to find it easy, to continue to support Industrial Mission. I mean also that this work has much about it that can be redolent of past years when the public sector was indeed public and government saw itself as there to help round the rough edges of insoluble disputes. Here in Industrial Mission is an instrument forged for engagement with the structures, and, lo and behold, the structures have lost interest, or been destroyed, or have just disappeared. I had the same sense when singing Fred Kaan's words about living and praying Magnificat '...in crowded street and council flat':[3] by the time we get around to it, there may not be any council flats left! Those organizations that retain an interest in Industrial Mission's work, such as trades unions, are themselves victims of so long a period of attrition that many young workers have no recollection at all of a time when the instruments of working class solidarity were honoured not just by their members but by society at large. Industrial Mission's pioneers rightly convicted the churches of their failure to enter that world of work. Yet the world Industrial Mission entered has, to a large extent, collapsed about its ears. Many of the papers in this collection and many of Industrial Mission's current initiatives bear witness to the vitality of the search for a new role, or the expression of the same task in a new world; but even as I salute that vitality I am conscious of the harsh reality within which it operates.

I must declare a few prejudices at the outset, so that you know where I am coming from. To do that I shall tell the story of a recent encounter with a longstanding friend, whose comments clarified for me the nature of the ground on which I stand. Despite a painful personal crisis, he said that what recently had caused him the most distress was the collapse of the communist regimes in Eastern Europe and the response of the

---

3.   See the last two lines of the well-known hymn by Fred Kaan, 'Sing me a Song of High Revolt': To Sing and live Magnificat/ In crowded street and council flat.

Communist Party (his party) in this country to those historic events. He described the weekend at which the CP was to meet to discuss its future. He was shattered to find that by the time he arrived on the Saturday morning the resolution to disband had already been put and carried. 'I don't understand,' he said to me, 'how you can hold to certain convictions all your life and then abandon your commitment just because of a setback, however great'. As often, it seemed to me that an avowedly non-religious person had put into words an understanding of the faithfulness at the heart of discipleship, and was expressing in a secular example much of what the experience of the exile and of the destruction of the Jerusalem Temple meant in terms of challenge to fundamental belief.

That experience increases my resolve to declare publicly that I find the widespread talk of the death or collapse of socialism both untrue and a particularly arrogant form of Western wishful thinking. It is utterly parochial, in that it bears no relation to the experience and longings of many in Western Europe or the exploitation which they suffer as a result of the virtual imposition of Western-led market thinking. Nor does it pay sufficient attention to the aspirations of countries of the two thirds world, many of which see no reason to change their political philosophy just because the particular form of that philosophy that was tried out in parts of Europe have come to grief.

As well as disdaining many of the current gloating obituaries for socialism, I also repent of much of my share in the depression of a decade and a half, during which it became very fashionable in political discussion, not least among people like me who were very sad about it, to say that it was the right that was generating all the ideas and setting the intellectual agenda of politics. It is certainly evident now, and should have been long ago, that the flurry of ideas that have translated themselves so quickly into legislation and executive action are basically variations on only one theme, the centrality of the market. The self-serving character of that theme, put about by people and nations who have everything to gain from it, is as clear as what it has added to the sum total of human misery.

Clear also, and so they should have been earlier, are the deceptions on which the proclamation of the end of socialism relies: a 'tight monetary policy', provided of course you do not take account of the horrendous escalation of personal debt, with all its enslaving social consequences; a 'rolling back of government', provided you do not notice the destruction of organs of local democratic authority or the construction, for example, of an education system which is controlled (by central government), not just as to its processes but far more seriously as to its content; the 'enfranchising of the individual', provided you are not too worried by the extent to which that the enfranchised's franchise is determined by their power in the market place. Much dialogue with the new right has simply served to enhance its credibility, to suggest that its intellectual content is more compelling than, in fact, it is. It is a highly self-serving ideology, designed to increase the resources of those who already have plenty of them. And while it may be important to listen to what those who support it have to say, we should do so with the motivation of Jesus: he did not hesitate to people his parables with crude capitalists, unscrupulous bankers, unjust stewards and so forth. The point he wished to make was not that they might be right, but rather that their opportunistic behaviour was at least as important for the supporters of the kingdom of God as it was for its opponents.

Therefore, the reconstruction of the organs of common life necessary for empowering the people is, as far as I am concerned, a central current challenge. The reinvigoration of our commitment to a just and sustainable commonwealth seems to me something for which Christians should pray and work. This may in part be because the experiment with a market-led politics, though it will go on and on, seems to me to be morally intolerable, a usurpation of power by those who already have too much of it for the good of their souls or the lives of their fellow human beings. It is also important to rebuild those organs of common life because of what it is to be a person, and what persons have been put into the world to do: to live in harmony with one another and to take our part, a constructive part and not a destructive one, in the care of the universe of created things.

To speak in this way, to be heard propounding the values of a Christian socialism, is to raise far more questions than are answered. They are incredibly complex and largely undiscovered mechanisms by which a nation, let alone a continent or a world, can regulate its life so as to give to persons and nations the best opportunity for the development of their talents and the exercise of their gifts and have their needs met. And we know from recent years that, if you get them wrong, people will quickly abandon the project in favour of political ideologies that appear to offer a more instant gratification of individuals' needs and wants—which is why the notion of a 'free market' came to look so attractive.

The development of the just and sustainable common life is immensely difficult. Huw Beynon was recently in Durham to give a summary of part of his history of the Durham miners. The history of the Durham miners is an important history, not least because there was a time when one quarter of all trades unionists were miners, and one quarter of all miners were in Durham. He told us how, at the time when the Durham coalfield was at its largest and most productive it had an almost unique shift system, one that relied on the fact that the women hardly ever went to sleep, but kept the fires burning and the water warm and food ready for their husbands and brothers and sons to return from their shift. I recall describing this to David Jenkins shortly before his retirement; he commented, 'Yes, it's a kind of slavery, isn't it; and the question is, can we do any better?' And so it is: can we do any better?

The contributors to the conference were, perhaps inevitably, entirely white. To counter-balance, I spent some of the off moments reading some items in the collection by Edwards and Dabydeen of eighteenth and nineteenth-century writings in English by black people;[4] it is every bit as harrowing, inspiring and demanding as some of the things which Anne Primavesi has put before us. I believe that slavery, and the way in which it is being recreated and encouraged by many present economic policies, is a very serious world issue; and I shall return to it later.

Whatever may be the evident and hidden complexities of a socialist project—the struggle to discover whether we *can* do any better—naming it in that way seems to me a vital first step. I am certainly interested in working and talking with those anxious to pursue that project. In that pursuit there are certainly to be found many problems that will need solving if we are to 'do any better'. And I believe it is essential that those pursuing that project should not allow themselves to be diverted by the self-denigrating sense that they need the help of people on the new right.

There is a sharp challenge in the statement from Henry Clark's book with which this paper opened. New social instruments must be developed, and yet the churches over the last decade and a half have often been identified as defending past instruments instead of recreating the vision of a social Britain. While the 'moderate incrementalism' of the churches' social pronouncements may have had its attractions, it has not projected the sense of our 'developing the vision of the Good Society and the theological rationale therefor'. This is evidenced in two recently published reports. The first is the Christian Aid report, *The Poor, the Gospel*

4.   P. Edwards and D. Dabydeen (eds.), *Black Writers in Britain 1760–1890* (Edinburgh: Edinburgh University Press, 1991).

and the Churches.[5] It reveals very clearly just how much work has to be done if Christian people in congregations are to be able to express their sense of need of a sustainable common life. The evidence is that attitudes to the poor which are primarily moralistic and individualistic are extremely prevalent, shown by the fact that what people say about the poor in this country is very different to their response to the poor overseas. The constant bombardment of people with pictures of the starving in Somalia and Ethiopia leads to their taking the view that the poor overseas 'can't help it', are 'victims', fitting objects for our generosity. On the other hand, the poor at home are felt to be 'layabouts', people who could help it if they tried. Neither picture, of course, bears much relation to the truth.

The other publication is a review, produced co-operatively by people from the universities in Sheffield and the University of Coventry, at the request of the Church Urban Fund. It is called *Hope in the City?*[6] It was a privilege, as part of my own research, to observe the progress of that research; and it reveals very clearly the shortcomings as well as the fruits of a social tradition which is primarily Anglican, although others have gone along with it. To read that is to be reminded of many of the sobering reflections that came my way when I was involved in the assessment of Industrial Mission.[7] Henry Clark's statement about the churches under Thatcher frames a conclusion to which we also came in looking at the various Industrial Mission teams. In some ways Industrial Mission participated to a fault in the virtues of that Anglican social tradition, and I found it interesting to learn that in one region the ecumenical body responsible for the oversight of Industrial Mission has made that overlap official by making the Church of England function as the 'lead denomination' in that area of work.

It seems to me that many of the assumptions in Ted Wickham's seminal book and in Leslie Hunter's thinking come from the traditions of a church with a view of itself as having an assured relationship with society at large and the responsibilities that flow from that.[8] So the call to set up

5. *The Poor, the Gospel and the Churches* (London: Christian Aid, 1994).

6. *Hope in the City?* (Sheffield: Sheffield Hallam University, 1994).

7. For the report of the working party, see *Industrial Mission—an Appraisal* (General Synod Board of Social Responsibility, 1988).

8. See E.R. Wickham, *Church and People in an Industrial City* (London: Lutterworth, 1957); and the collection of essays about Bishop Hunter, G. Hewitt (ed.), *Strategist for the Spirit: Leslie Hunter, Bishop of Sheffield 1939–1962* (Oxford: Becket Publications, 1985).

Industrial Mission was in many ways a call to take seriously that commitment to the whole of society. For that very reason what followed from the call has often lacked the robustness either of the Roman Catholic official pronouncements, to which David McLellan refers in his paper, or the English dissenting traditions, which would have a different view of what would be involved in getting alongside working people. My sense is that when Anglicans (and I write as one) are faced with a choice between their assured place in society and a commitment to the poor or to working class people, they will always, after much agonising, choose the former. For example the recent flurry of debate, yet again, about the rights and wrongs of establishment has been marked by numerous comments to the effect that setting up some review of the details of the relationship between Church and state would 'send the wrong signals'; I ask myself, to whom? And, about what? So one of the most important questions Industrial Mission has to address to us is, could we ever make a different choice, if we were confronted, as we so often are, between our assured and comfortable relationship with 'the whole of society' on the one hand, and our commitment to its poorest and most marginalized members on the other?

It seems to me that the 'human rights' tradition here too reveals a major deficiency. For it is clear, to take a recent and apparently domestic discussion within the Church of England as an example, that a church that votes for the ordination of women on the basis of a rights tradition is likely (as has been shown) to spend a disproportionate amount of time on the rights of the people who disagree. On the other hand, a church which had decided that the issue of the ordination of women was an issue of the uncontrolled and unfettered freedom of God would have to accept that it was now ordaining women because of an awareness that in the past it had rejected a *gift from God*, something which, I dare to say, is an even more serious thing to do than to offend the rights of women.[9] Once the Church had done that it would have to have some painful conversations about what it would mean also to regard as a gift those unable to accept the decision; but that is a very different conversation from one about their 'rights'. Similarly the problem about the 'incrementalist' attempt to address the issues of poverty on the basis of the rights of the poor is that while it may seek to ameliorate the roughest consequences of the Thatcherite project, it has not engaged in the construction of a vision of what a society would be like if it were predicated on the uncontrolled

9.   See my book, *BeLonging* (London: SPCK, 1991).

and unfettered freedom of God to choose whom God chooses, to have mercy on whom God has mercy and therefore, to give precedence to the needs of the poor over the wants of the already well off.

I now turn to something else which has been apparent from the seminar papers, and which needs to be brought centre stage. Anne Primavesi has said a great deal about debt and the slavery that is being imposed on countries as a result of the mounting burden of debt; and I have found that the writings of black people during the period of slavery make deeply disturbing reading. But when the cut in student grants and the increase in student loans was announced last autumn, I found, because I am a student's parent, that I was addressed through my own self-interest with some very searching questions. It suddenly became clear to me that what was going on was an exercise in social control, in that the position of debtor is in sharp contrast to the position of the person who is the recipient of the free mercy of God. Debt, as an instrument of social control, is obviously around in questions of student finance, because if one thing is certain it is that the increase in student loans and student indebtedness will do a great deal to prevent anything like the disturbances of 1968 happening again: people with a large debt tend to behave themselves (unless the debt gets so large that they have nothing to lose—which is why a real collapse in the property market will not be allowed to happen).

When, however, we notice that aspect of student indebtedness, we need also to notice two other things as well: first, the so-called increase in home ownership is actually an increase in private indebtedness; and private indebtedness is an instrument of social control, no less than international indebtedness is a means to the control of small and poor nations. Secondly, that the reduction to slavery of our Hebrew forbears was not, as has happened to the slaves of the last three hundred years, a story of invasion, colonisation and kidnapping, resulting in slavery, but was the result of something very like debt. You will recall that when Joseph's brothers had no food they asked him for some, and he demanded payment. They handed over their money, and thus lost their immediate liquidity. The second year they had no food and no money, and he demanded their cattle and thus took away their medium term liquidity. Finally, they had no food, and now no money or cattle, and their own bodies were demanded and they became slaves.

That is why in the Bible and in the Christian tradition there are strict rules about lending at interest; it is why we read ordinances about the years of jubilee, and why there are rules about continuing to lend even in the sixth year. It is why the Jewish community has rules about not charging interest to people who are in need, and it is why debt must rank as one of the most serious social issues. I regard Jesus Christ as *redeemer*, that is the one who writes off your mortgage. That is what makes him dangerous; for if all debtors had their debts written off tomorrow morning, who knows what kind of anarchy would break loose? For who knows to what extent people are controlled by their place in the debt economy. In seeking to present Jesus as redeemer to the world there are surely the serious issues as to what that kind of gospel would mean in the face of the huge, and for some highly profitable, burden of debt that is around.

To rebuild a social vision, means, therefore, taking a new view of something like debt. For example, quite contrary to the rhetoric of the last fifteen years, it is *public* debt that is the only really morally defensible kind of debt. For it is quite defensible for a community to decide that in the interest of improving some aspect of its common life or dealing with some pressing social problem, it will forego some of its present resources; that is what borrowing is. Public borrowing is asking people who have resources which they do not require at the present to put them into a shared pool which can be used for the common good. That is an entirely proper view of debt, part of God's project of inviting us to share together, to plan together, for the creation of a just and sustainable common life. Contrary again to the rhetoric of the last fifteen years we are not to distrust our planning and assume that the only way our common life can be created is for it to emerge from the pretended freedom of customers in the market place. So the building of a social vision, a vision of society, is crucially important; as Henry Clark points out, there are no grounds for believing that such a vision can be drawn from an already existing public consensus.

That brings me to a further assumption that seems to have been around, to a degree, in the story of Industrial Mission, and to have been exemplified in the painful story of confrontation which can be found in the history of the Sheffield Industrial Mission. When conducting the appraisal of Industrial Mission to which I have referred, a group came to Sheffield. In the course of that visit we spoke with a number of church leaders, among them the present Bishop of Sheffield, David Lunn. He commented in our conversation with him that there seemed to have been an assumption hidden in the origins of Industrial Mission that there was latent in working people a kind of religious belief, indeed a latent Christianity, which, if the Church would only get alongside them, would surface without the need for explicit proclamation and conversion. He thought the assumption a mistaken one, and I think that the history of recent times suggests that it is indeed mistaken. First of all, people have an increasingly shallow grasp, if any, of the Christian history which those involved in the churches and in Industrial Mission, take for granted: its stories, its actions, its rituals and its meanings. To assume that an understanding of these things lies hidden under the surface may be very dangerous, not least because, as seen in recent racial conflicts in East London, there are other things lying rather near the surface too. Therefore the need for explicit witness and communication, and the conveying of the stories and images to people at a level of depth that will gain their allegiance and touch their feelings remains an extremely important area of work. Part of the polarization between the churches' residential ministry and activities like Industrial Mission is the tragedy of the coming apart of two deeply connected enterprises, the building of a social vision on the one hand, and on the other, the communication of deep aspects of our Christian inheritance which will be needed to sustain that vision in the hearts of people.

What we have to take very seriously is the need, in the development of a sustainable common life and the social instruments that will promote it, of a good and wholesome rhetoric. David McLellan referred in his paper to people's religious feelings, and the importance of people having the right religious feelings. That seems to me to be a very important insight, not demanding some tight orthodoxy, but requiring the recognition that Industrial Mission is in the business of good rhetoric, of accessing people's deepest convictions about the nature of life and the purpose of human existence.

This is the business of a search for rhetoric, not just the rhetoric of justice, but the search for images, feelings, religious sensibilities that will nourish and sustain the search for justice when it is faced with the destructive rhetoric of which we have all too much recent experience. Sue Havens's paper is very important in this regard, insofar as it is about gaining access to those aspects of people's lives which only religion can reach. About that, those concerned to press the need for a developed social vision must be much more up front and open if we are to avoid arousing only a skin-deep and incomplete allegiance to whatever social vision we succeed in developing.

I come now to my concluding point, made not as a criticism of the way in which this conference was organized, which was intended for its particular purpose. I have, however, a perception about such conferences as this, namely that they are part of an essentially liberal enterprise. Insofar as there are differences of view here they are allowed to come out in dissipated ways, in seminar groups and private conversation; we did not manage to create a structure in which the severity of the conflicts which all of us are acquainted with in everyday life would come out into the open among us. The familiar structure of seminars, papers, lecture inputs and question times is one that builds more than we would like to believe on the assumptions that Henry Clark criticises, and which I mentioned at the beginning, of an assured social consensus.

Within that consensus and within such a structure you can of course hear radical and inspiring insights, as was our good fortune here, and sharp challenges such as appear in Anne Primavesi's lecture. But what the development of a social vision and its sustaining rhetoric also require is a structure that engages us, in a way that involves the possibility of hurt, in the conflicts and polarizations which have featured so much in IMSY's history and will most certainly feature in any attempt on our part to forge again the instruments we need for a just common life. Such are the conflicts which have to be resolved if we are to develop 'the vision of the Good Society', and which have to be engaged if we are to work together for what I still name as God's socialist project, which is what I believe we are called to do.

So a rhetoric, and an experiential enactment of the conflicts and polarisations involved in that project, seem to me what we require if we are to engage society and Church in the pursuit of that corporate vision. That combination is also proper for us in particular. It is proper for a group of people founded upon the event of the enactment of God's rhetoric, of the rhetoric becoming flesh. That was how it was when God interrupted the rhetoric of destructiveness with a rhetoric made flesh, and thereby gave us both a rhetoric and an experiential enactment of what the building of the human project would be like.

INDUSTRIAL CULTURE AND HUMAN VALUES: INDIVIDUALISM IN A TEAM CULTURE

James Hall

What follows is in no way meant to be a conclusive piece of academic research, but simply the observations of one who is curious and yet disturbed by the changing culture in British industry. These observations are based on contacts with a number of individuals, groups, agencies (eg. Welsh Development Agency), trades unions, managements and companies in South Wales (mainly Mid and South Glamorgan).

The Issue

> We are all made of many parts; no man is singular in the way he lives his life. He only lives it fully in relation to others. (Keenan 1993: 277)

Brian Keenan's book is far more than a simple account of his nightmare as a hostage in Lebanon; it is the story of an intensely personal journey into a painful and yet rewarding self-understanding. A central part of this journey is his relationships with fellow prisoners *and* his captors. For me, the book was riveting, painful, funny and full of unobtrusive and accidental (!) theology (as the above quote illustrates—reminiscent of 1 Corinthians 12). I begin here because this story (a classic, I believe) is, for me, a good example of the need to face oneself as an individual in the light of relationships with others. It is *only* in such relating that the deepest parts of the personal journey can be experienced according to Keenan. He is not alone in this idea.

> The Greek New Testament is full of 'syn' words, stressing the togetherness of Christians with Christ and with one another. The Christian faith therefore stresses not only the importance of each person but also of that person finding his personhood in a community of persons. (Preston 1979: 70)

I believe that in British industrial culture there is a basic dichotomy between individualism and teamwork. There are, of course, many histories and complexities in modern industrial life. For this essay I wish to be very narrow and look at individualism and team culture in certain contexts.

Some Aspects of Team Culture

To state the obvious, British industry is no longer at the centre of the industrial world. For much of the latter part of this century, however, it appears to have been acting as if it were and retaining models of organization and working patterns which were developed in its heyday. This has included an emphasis on strong demarcation between roles within the workplace and a confrontational style of industrial relations. Many people on all 'sides' of industry have now repudiated such ideas for a number of reasons—not least because the old ways were not producing enough profits and/or jobs.

The obvious question to ask is: 'What do others do?' In the industries I visit the most common source of inspiration is Japanese systems. 'Just in Time' and 'Total Quality Management' are the phrases most often heard on my rounds. The Japanese have developed an approach 'preached' by Dr Edwards Deming from the United States who visited Japan in 1950 to share his insights (it is difficult to avoid religious language when referring to this subject). Both the above systems are designed to gain more profit for a company, thus securing its place in the market in the face of competition.

Just in Time (JIT)

'Just in Time' is a system designed to eliminate waste wherever it occurs—including materials, time, handling operations, over-production and machinery. The idea is to *prevent* waste rather than to *cure* it. All the basic assumptions of traditional British industry are questioned. For example, the notion that a company must carry large amounts of stock and completed goods is discarded in JIT theory. JIT, put simply, means that materials coming into a factory arrive 'just in time' to be used in manufacture. This requires a good relationship with suppliers so that stock can be called in as and when needed. Often this good relationship, based on quality and price, will mean single sourcing. Materials on shelves equals dead money, lower productivity, less profit. This philosophy is followed throughout the process until the goods or services are with the customer. In fact, each part of the process in the company has a 'customer' (e.g., the production line is a customer of goods inwards). The rest of JIT revolves around this philosophy to enable the smoothest possible flow with the least possible waste. Obviously, each company has variations to match the products and services provided, but the principles are the same. When parts cannot flow in one continuous line and they need to be moved to another area of the factory, a system called Kanban (Japanese for 'ticket') is used. This creates small stock areas next to the following process—just enough to avoid stopping the process. When the stock reaches a certain level, it is replenished using a ticket system which simply shuttles between 'customer' and 'supplier' in the factory as and when necessary. Each 'customer', therefore, orders just enough materials for the order he or she must supply to the next 'customer'.

In JIT, tasks should be simpler, nearer to hand and 'owned' by those performing them; those working in each area should feel they have some stake in what is happening. To improve performance and eliminate waste JIT usually involves calling together multi-level teams (Continuous Improvement Teams) to examine and recommend changes. Who does the calling, who is included and what power these teams have will vary with the commitment or otherwise of management to following JIT all the way. From what I have observed, this is the rub—you cannot sit on the fence with JIT. The system requires every department to work this way because it is based on the flow of work throughout the plant. Without management commitment JIT is a lost cause and merely a cosmetic exercise, and many in industry fear this *is* the case. People should be selected for the teams from every section of the area where JIT is implemented (probably a pilot scheme at first), and the team needs a variety of perspectives. Some managers take the view that only those who are initially co-operative should be asked to take part. This can have the undesired effect of further alienating those who are already unhappy with management or the process for whatever reason. The more risky way is to include some who will be highly sceptical; risky because the scheme may be sabotaged before it starts. However, JIT relies on people at every level taking a different approach and without the sceptics seeing the proposals working (or otherwise) nothing may happen.

Traditional JIT puts great emphasis on team work to examine problems, face challenges, motivate, train and lead people. Teams are more than the sum of the parts; in problem solving teams are almost always better than individuals; joint solutions are more likely to have a wider ownership than individual ones. It is fascinating to see the religious language which is used in JIT manuals when speaking about the people in teams:

> It doesn't matter too much if the people you have in mind are initially not interested in JIT or don't *believe* that it will work. Once they have seen what can be done, some truly amazing *conversions* are observed. In fact, as with other aspects of life, some of the best enthusiasts start out as *disbelievers*. Given an open mind, though, the results will soon speak for themselves and you will have gained not just a *convert* but a *disciple* eager to *preach* the *message* to others. (Wheatley 1992: 32; my emphasis)

Total Quality Management (TQM)
Allied to JIT is Total Quality Management. With the drastically reduced lead times of JIT there is much less slack in the system and, therefore, less room for poor quality products. As JIT tries to reduce any buffer of products to zero, each item must be right first time to satisfy the customer. The emphasis on quality moves from goods being inspected at the end of a process to the actual manufacture. Quality must be *built into* a product. Again, this requires team work. Each member of a production cell or working unit must feel that they have a stake in the process and, therefore, take responsibility for the quality of their operation. Motivation has often been via piece-work and bonus systems: the more you can produce, the more you are paid. Many factories still use this. Two main difficulties arise: first, this can lead to over-production (what is the point of building thousands of units when the customer has only ordered a few hundred?); secondly, quality is usually the first casualty in such systems. TQM believes that no-one likes producing defective goods and that, given a chance, most people want to take a pride in their work. The team element comes in the relating needed between people in the process. TQM teaches that it is preferable to have a *product* orientated cell of production as opposed to a *process* orientated cell. In practice this should mean that the next process in manufacture is literally only an arm's length away. The quality of one's work will then be seen to affect one's immediate neighbour, and not some faceless department. If a problem arises, it can be sorted out between members of the team who are all in the same room contributing to the same product. Another advantage promoted by TQM is that workers can see the end product which should, in turn, help them all feel a part of the creative process. Obviously, I have described the ideal scenario.

Corporate Identity

In every company I visit there appears to have been an increased level of activity surrounding corporate identity. By this I mean a higher profile for the company name and image among employees and in the community (local or international). A well known example of this (but not a company I visit) is BP, which spent £1 million on its new logo. The idea appears to be to promote a sense of 'all being together in this venture'. In many large companies employees can buy or are given products with the company logo. Sponsorship and local public relations share a high profile. It is crucial to be known and recognized as a quality company which cares for people and the community. This has been particularly noticeable in the privatized utilities who have been forced to go through a form of death and resurrection into the 'new life' of the private sector. (Some would, of course, actually want to use such language about the brave new age of 'leaner, fitter' utilities.) This was a painful process in the Electricity Supply Industry (with which I am involved), for instance. It meant shedding the years of deeply held commitments to public service and taking on the mantle of a company whose main purpose must be to stay in business by making a profit and keeping the shareholders happy. I remember being at a presentation where employees were told in an 'evangelical' speech that CEGB people were *yesterday's* people. Now employees must begin again in the new world of the privatized company and not cling to the past (echoes of Second Isaiah). The sense of communal bereavement in this situation should not be underestimated (an important area of pastoral ministry for Industrial Mission which should always interact with the prophetic). This change, whether it is seen as good or bad in the long run, had the effect of negating the value of much that had gone on before and, by implication, devaluing the people who came from the CEGB—'yesterday's people'.

Many companies now have 'Mission Statements' and 'People Values Statements' which are meant to spell out the overall direction of the business and the valuing of people as the business's 'greatest asset'. The positive side can be that, sometimes for the first time, a company takes an overall look at where it wants to go—away from the rat-race of production. It is also quite a challenge for employers and employees to have actually written down how they should treat one another. I cannot help noticing, however, that these statements have increased in usage at a time of recession and when many companies are 'down-sizing' (or, to sanitize it further, '*right*-sizing'). It is almost as though companies are trying to convince themselves that they are not *that* bad after all, even though they have made *x* number of people redundant or continue to pay low wages. Is there a sense of guilt here? Sometimes I have noticed some improvement in the way people are treated (often with a change in management); is this a form of atonement?

Corporate identity, from the company's point of view, is about belonging and feeling a part of the wider organization. It is about being happy to be associated with the company—wearing the company T-shirt outside work as well as inside!

3. Some Criticisms of Team Culture

Corporate Identity

As you can see, I have already started to question the notion of 'corporate identity' as it is worked out in many companies. Many employees are highly sceptical of the associated hype. What matters to them is the reality of how *they* are treated day to day. So often, I am told, these statements are made by well meaning (not all) managers at the top but are not followed by those between top management and staff. Sometimes this is simply because the 'them' and 'us' syndrome is still deeply rooted. Other times it is because middle management have the unpalatable task of 'letting people go' (another euphemism) and then trying to convince those that are left, with the same amount of work to do but fewer staff, that they (the management) are 'people friendly'. Much pastoral time has been spent with these middle managers who are often under immense pressure.

JIT and TQM

Because of the obvious linkage between JIT and TQM, I will list my criticisms under the same heading.

a. *Positive.* There can be a greater awareness of others in the organization. There is a recognition that every skill is vital to the overall purpose of the business. The traditionally dictatorial style of management which simply says, 'Do it this way, because I am the manager and, therefore, am right', should go under JIT/TQM. Everyone should be 'empowered' (Pentecostal?) to think and act without always having to refer back. Only the team should 'fail' and not individuals—and, anyway, failure should be seen as part of the pathway to ultimate success.

b. *Negative*. With the emphasis on being 'company people' there is often not enough room for healthy dissent. For some 'converts' to these systems, it is as though the sceptics were trying to wreck the company if they question JIT/TQM. When all is said and done, this is a system to make more profit for the company first and foremost; not a change of people values. One always needs to ask questions of the company as a whole: Who benefits from greater profits? Who has a stake in the company's success? Are employees really allowed to participate in decision making or is it a sham? How open and approachable are management? To be fair, in one company I visit there is now a lot more information shared about the company's performance, all employees are also shareholders and all seem to be listened to at a local level. But this appears to be rare.

What role do the unions have in this? Sometimes such systems are a way of weakening them by going directly to the work-force and ignoring the importance of corporate negotiating. Approached as individuals, employees feel vulnerable and will often agree to a course of action just to avoid conflict and a potential loss of status or employment. With a union or works council approach there can be more honesty about the issues when individuals feel less threatened. There is also a danger that 'good company people' are picked for the teams in JIT/TQM, thus avoiding conflict in the short-term but, almost inevitably, creating trouble for the future. Also, people are often reluctant to join a team for fear of being ostracised by other staff for joining in a 'management scheme'. Making JIT/TQM something that really challenges management *and* work force is not easy and requires *courage* and *trust* on all sides. JIT/TQM are not designed to challenge the overall structure of market-led capitalism and yet there are seeds of a critique: for example, the emphasis on co-operation and not confrontation.

The religious language noted above is surely no mistake. People are expected to 'convert' to the systems lock, stock and barrel, to 'sell their soul to the company'. I am always wary of any ideology which demands total submission or obedience (Christianity, as a religion, included). For me, there is no place in industry, church or world for 'hanging one's brain up at the door'. I have recently met one individual who has been through such a conversion. It is frightening to hear him being so utterly convinced that thenew way is absolutely right. He even worries management!

Some Aspects of Individualism

The last fifteen years have seen an explosion in the proclaiming of and, for some, the practice of individual 'freedom of choice'. The Thatcher years have introduced the 'right' to buy your council house, the 'right' to choose a school for your children, the 'right' not to belong to a trades union, the emasculating of trades union power via key disputes and legislation, and (perhaps above all) the encouragement and legitimizing of individual gain. There is much more, and there are plenty of others who have produced careful critiques of this momentous period. I mention it simply as a backcloth for my observations as a practitioner in Industrial Mission. I believe that many people in society have been 'converted' to a 'creed of greed' which keeps enough people happy to sustain a Conservative government, but has created a growing unemployed or low paid underclass which cannot usually benefit from these new 'rights', because they often involve opportunities provided by greater income (e.g., living in more expensive areas where there is greater choice). Industry does not operate in a vacuum. I want to mention several aspects of individualism in business today.

Personal Contracts
These have been increasing in a number of companies, especially for middle management and above. Contracts are drawn up which reflect an individual's personal work and 'worth'. This can be good, in that employees are more aware of their particular responsibilities and, therefore, feel a greater sense of pride in *their* work, as opposed simply to contributing to the workplace. On the other hand, personal contracts split the employee from colleagues, who may not know what he or she is contracted to do or how much he or she is being paid. Unions and professional associations are thereby circumvented because negotiations with employers over terms, conditions and pay are no longer relevant. The wider services of such corporate bodies are therefore limited. Personal contracts are often linked to a time scale, which can also put great pressure on individuals to 'keep in' with management for fear of non-renewal. 'Fixed term contracts' can be healthy in that they give a review date for employer and employee, but so much depends on the goodwill and fair practice of an employer. The onus and power have shifted. Some organizations operate very short-term contracts (e.g., 3 months for workers in the mental health service in one local health

authority in South Wales). A price is available on everything, it seems. In some companies, each activity is priced and matched to a person who is costed to perform the tasks. There is often little room for people to be 'carried' by others in times of crisis—a job needs doing and if *x* cannot do it *y* will be bought in instead. Personal contracts of all sorts tend to force people into being 'company people'; dissent is frowned upon. I know of some personal contracts which contain a phrase to the effect that, with four weeks' notice, any part of the contract may be altered at the company's discretion. What is its value here, I ask, if it is so easy to change? Doesn't the word 'contract' imply agreement by both parties? The same company, incidentally, discourages any conversation about personal contracts among staff.

Contracting Out

Others are not employed, but brought in as contractors—they are self-employed, paid a gross amount and the business has no obligations in terms of national insurance, sickness, pension or redundancy. Some top earners do very well out of this (as freelancers), but many do not earn enough to have any financial security. This can put an unbearable strain on people and their families, but is part of an overall drift to the casual-izing of labour. There are a number of theories on this, but I tend to favour the 'core—periphery' argument which says that industry is moving towards employing a small number of professionals and techni-cians directly (usually paying them well) and the supporting services via contracts (for instance, cleaning and security) (see Ormiston and Ross 1990: 43). I have seen this happen in several places. Quite often the same people who were employed by a company for cleaning or security are re-employed by the firm which wins the contract and usually pays a lot less. Some people are on 'zero hours' contracts: they are called in as and when necessary, but the employer has no obligation to provide set hours.

The firm's objective is to cut costs. Putting work out to contract is almost bound, therefore, to reduce the wages and conditions of employees. I know this to be a fact on one site I visit.

Performance Related Pay (PRP)

There are varieties of PRP but the same god to be served—perform-ance. The schemes I have come across deal with the fringe benefit level of pay, whether someone receives more or less than the annual pay award. This is measured in a number of ways depending on the nature of the business. Usually, targets are set by management or supervisors and the individual is assessed on the attainment of these targets and on overall initiative and diligence.

One positive outcome is that people are forced to look at their own performance and to be honest with themselves. This can be particularly helpful in large organizations where it is easier to pass the buck or for others to take the credit for one's own hard work.

Sometimes the systems to measure PRP can be very complicated, particularly when the business is complex. It is very difficult, for instance, to measure teachers in a school setting. Surely it is not just about exam results? What about the standards of pupils coming into the school, social background, other staff who may be motivating or otherwise? Just how do you measure the vital area of teacher–pupil relationships? Can it ever be objective enough to be measured? These questions apply to many other working environments, especially where relationships of trust and team-work are involved.

PRP is in marked tension with the team culture described above. How can a single member working in a TQM environment be singled out if the whole philosophy is based on the team owning the work, success and failure? One of the principle team-breaking effects of PRP I have noticed is the inevitable rivalry and jealousy generated by some people being awarded more than others. Management and supervisors also have a hard job maintaining relationships of trust and openness when it is they who have to sit down with individuals to decide pay levels. In one place I visit most people will admit privately that the gain of a few pounds in pay has been far out-weighed by the loss of trust and the jealousy between team members and between teams.

PRP tends to complicate the JIT/TQM scene by splitting people away from their teams and by introducing a layer of bureaucracy into a system that is designed to do away with waste. It is interesting to note that several companies such as Shell have considered PRP and backed away from it for some of these reasons.

Self-Employment

There has been a huge rise in the number of small businesses alongside the demise of many larger employers. Self-employment is a major part of this and has been actively encouraged by government. In some ways, this has been covered under the section on contracting out. The words themselves—'Self', 'Employment'—are significant because they illustrate a cultural shift for many people away from a corporate culture to one of individual enterprise which will make or break them personally. Many have lost homes as well as businesses in their attempts to be self-employed. For most it is a tough option. The key, it seems, when looking at self-employment in the context of personal contracts is that the 'risk' element in business has moved its centre of gravity towards the contractor or self-employed business. Larger employers do not want to have the responsibility for employing people; they want to make a profit by successfully bringing together the resources of materials, capital and labour (I have grossly over-generalized to make a point). This is illustrated by the slide from 'Personnel' to 'Human Resources' when talking about the people part of this equation. All the contractors, self-employed and casual labour are seen as a resource like a raw material to be taken off the shelf as and when necessary.

There are two things that strike me as sad here: (1) that people are devalued; (2) that some companies are short-sighted enough to believe that it does not matter how you treat people, as long as there is some immediate result. In fact, companies themselves seem to be taking on this individualism that is rampant in society, only caring for themselves and yet actually not doing so because they seem to miss the point that the only way to get quality from a work-force is to treat it with quality.

Human Values?

There are three strands for my final comments:

The Reality of the Modern World

Individualism, in the sense of being able to stand on one's own two feet and not having to rely on anyone else is, in today's modern Western culture, a denial of reality. This, for me, was best illustrated by a visit to National Grid Control, the nerve centre for all Britain's electricity supply. Society would not function without electricity—public or private. Very few people or industries have the ability or finance (much less the desire) to generate their own power. They have to rely on others who generate, supply and sell electricity, who in their turn rely on a variety of fuel supplies, and so the chain continues backwards and forwards. The fact that there are now more contractual arrangements holding all this together actually illustrates the need for agreements between individuals and groups in society. We cannot do without one another even if we wanted to. One of the problems of modern living is that many of us have been lulled into a false sense of individual self-sufficiency. It is as though the trappings of late twentieth-century consumerism have cocooned us from the reality of how we came by such luxuries. It is worth trying to reflect just how many people and organizations are involved in bringing you your washing machine—and then the electricity to run it, the water to fill it and the powder and softener to use in it.

A Christian View of Humanity
Please note the indefinite article. This is simply a personal sketch. In his challenging book, 'Christianity and the Market', John Atherton quotes B.F. Westcott:

> Individualism and Socialism correspond with opposite views of humanity. Individualism regards humanity as made up of disconnected or warring atoms; Socialism regards it as an organic whole, a vital unity formed by the combination of contributory members mutually interdependent. It follows that Socialism differs from Individualism both in method and aim. The method of Socialism is co-operation, the method of Individualism is competition... The aim of Socialism is the fulfilment of service, the aim of Individualism is the attainment of some personal advantage... (Atherton 1992: 183)

Atherton quotes Westcott criticizing his lack of understanding of real socialism. Leaving that aside; if we were to replace 'socialism' with 'community', the point can be well made that a purely individualistic approach to life brings a disconnectedness which sometimes leads to war, and competition which can lead to personal gain at someone else's expense. Not only does the world not operate like this, many Christians would argue that this is not the *right* way to operate. There are a number of questions regarding the use of self interest for the common good (thus reflecting the falleness of humanity, perhaps also the need to love ourselves before our neighbours), but selfishness—the making of individual gain into a god—cannot ring true with a faith that proclaims such an overwhelming and boundless generosity. The good news of Jesus Christ is nothing if not about God's selfless giving of God's own being. Many theologians (e.g., Moltmann) have helped us to see that the idea of 'community', a vital connectedness that comes with being human, is not simply an *adjunct* to the Christian faith, but *essentially a part of it.* We do not believe in its importance simply because Jesus called together an odd collection of followers, but because of the overwhelming sense of belonging between Father/Mother, Son and Spirit *in* God. In other words, God does not only *create* community, God *is* community and, in inviting us to be part of the kingdom, God invites us to be more fully *human* (for me, part of the incredible meaning of incarnation), more fully in communion with God and one another. Much individualistic piety is a construct of nineteenth-century Victorian religion (influenced, of course, by the Enlightenment). R.H. Preston points out that for an individual to be truly free he or she must acknowledge the society which is prior to that individual—into which they were born, the setting within which an individual can be free (Preston 1979: 73ff.). Atherton's book illustrates that there is much complexity when it comes to working this out in practice. He opts for a socially aware system of market economics as the least harmful way (the only way according to him). Others have looked at the same data and decided otherwise. It is not my purpose to enter this economic debate here, except to agree with Preston and Atherton about the importance of humanity belonging together and the challenges with which we are faced.

The Good News?

I believe that the most important 'good news' for today's atomizing world is this community found in God in the world. One sign of hope among many is the increasing need for people to identify with movements for change (e.g., green issues) and the generosity of so many in the face of human tragedy (as I write, the Rwanda holocaust is grabbing the headlines). Some of this is undoubtedly self-interest, an acknowledgement that if we in the wealthy West do not do something for the desperate plight of so many people and for this planet, we will all go down together. But I do not think this is the whole story. It has always impressed me that some of the largest amounts collected for Ethiopia in 1984–85 were in the mining communities of the South Wales Valleys, which were so hit by the year long strike, and not in the wealthy suburbs of Cardiff.

It is interesting to note that so much team language has entered industry from another culture. While we must be critical—both of the motivation behind its use and the values implied in it—this team culture can be much nearer the kingdom than the harsh individualism which has thrived and been encouraged in our own culture.

I was asked to contribute something because I am a Baptist. Many accuse us of being overtly individualistic. This criticism is often justified.

One classic example has been the over emphasis on individual con-version and personal witness in the act of baptism itself (believers, of course), as opposed to the corporate act of the Church in baptizing another person into the body of Christ. In the last century this tradition, heavily influenced by Victorian individualism and the Protestant work ethic, had almost forgotten its own roots. In the seventeenth century Baptists in the UK, as part of the Separatist movement, felt compelled to leave the established Church because of their view of the New Testament Church as the gathered *community* of believers. Early Baptists (especially the General Baptists) would not contemplate the later forms of individual isolationism. Although every person in the church community should be a believer (by personal conviction—Baptists have often been in the fore-front of the fight for individual rights), they were only thus in relation-ship with one another and, through the church meeting, with other like-minded fellowships (which formed Associations long before the Baptist Union) (see White's book).

I finish with a quote from one of my Baptist 'heroes':

> As long as there is poverty in the world I can never be rich, even if I have a billion dollars. As long as diseases are rampant and millions of people in this world cannot expect to live more than twenty-eight or thirty years, I can never be totally healthy, even if I just got a good check-up at Mayo Clinic. I can never be what I ought to be until you are what you ought to be. This is the way our world is made. No individual or nation can stand out boasting of being independent. We are interdependent. (King 1984: 21)

Select Bibliography

Atherton, J., *Christianity and the Market* (London: SPCK, 1992).

Keenan, B., *An Evil Cradling* (New York: Vintage Books, 1993).

King, C.S, *The Words of Martin Luther King* (London: Robson, 1984).

Ormiston, H., and D.M. Ross (eds.), *New Patterns of Work* (Edinburgh: Saint Andrew Press), 1990

Preston, R.H., *Religion and the Persistence of Capitalism* (London: SCM Press, 1979).

Wheatley, M., *Understanding Just In Time* (Headway Series; London: Hodder & Stoughton, 1992).

White, B.R., *The English Baptists of the 17th Century* (London: Baptist Historical Society, 1983).

Industrial Mission as Prophecy: An Invitation to Poetry

Sue Havens

Walter Brueggemann argues that the establishment of the davidic dynasty, and the temple theology characteristic of Jerusalem at the time of its fall (587 BCE) constituted a time of cultural and theological malaise which parallels that of our own society as the inheritors of the Enlightenment—including the Church which is situated within it.[1] Society in both periods, buttressed by the religious establishment, represents a patriarchal authority which protects the interests of a wealthy and powerful establishment and disempowers and impoverishes a significant population. Such a religious establishment, then as now and regardless of its religious claims, engages in idolatry through the service of wealth. It is antithetical to the service of God and can only be challenged by an alternative understanding of human faith and the action of God. The prophetic task, first and foremost in such a world, is to create space for God's conversion of his people. To meet his vocation, the prophet takes his stance for God from within the community of the people by means of a faith-filled articulation of tradition which brings about a new possibility.

As I read Brueggemann, I became increasingly aware that the world of prophet and crisis in Jerusalem and Exile is remarkably like my own. I am persuaded that the church communities of the twentieth century are as convicted and paralysed in themselves and in relation to society as those of the Temple, because our theology and practice is bankrupt. It seems to me that our world needs prophets like Jeremiah, Ezekiel and Second Isaiah; and that industrial missioners might be those prophets, but that we consistently fail so to be. I asked myself how the Church practises its idolatry, why industrial missioners fail to be its prophets, and how we might exercise our ministry so as to become truly prophetic.

To the extent that the Church attempts to take seriously economic issues, from the perspective of God's desire at least for equity, it does so

---

1. W. Brueggemann, *Hopeful Imagination* (Philadelphia: Fortress Press, 1986).

from a position within the system and in the main without sufficient systemic analysis. The Church responds in this way, not through a conscious will to do evil, but from a variety of very human defences of self-interest. The first of these defences is the elaboration of a tradition which claims 'spiritual adherence' (as though it can be divorced from sharp, effective action for justice), clear and nurtured membership of worshipping groups and personal piety as the chief issues of holiness.[2] It is a tradition we share with Jerusalem. The second is our desire that faith should be comfortable. We live in a postmodern, complex, pluralistic world which confuses us, isolates us and seems to create and justify the private spheres of life as the only ones where we can exercise any (and only limited) control. The pressures of existence tend to relegate the practice of religion to domestic life, which we desire to be safe.[3] Any Christian teaching or preaching that pushes us out into religiously convicted economic action also pushes us out into that complex and painful public world, where the light shines on our advantage and implication in existing oppressive systems and where we must struggle to learn new ways. We are brought to a learning horizon, which is always painful. Faced with the pain, we can struggle to overcome it and find alternatives. We can develop approaches which seem to move us into new and creative commitments, but actually keep us safe;[4] or we can snuggle back into the security of the earlier state of limited awareness and try to stay comfortable.[5] The result is that a conservative Church does not attempt

2.   *The Gospel, the Poor and the Churches* (London: Christian Aid, 1994).

3.   J.M Hull, *What Prevents Christian Adults from Learning?* (Philadelphia: Trinity Press International, 1991), especially ch. 3, 'The Need to be Right and the Pain of Learning'. Also J. Fowler, *Faith Development and Pastoral Care* (Philadelphia: Fortress Press, 1987), pp. 63ff. for summary of Stage 3, 'Synthetic Conventional Faith and the Interpersonal Self.'

4.   *The Gospel, the Poor and the Churches*. The report demonstrates that frequently churches which do concern themselves with poverty are more inclined to focus on Third World poverty than on First World poverty. They have a more benign and sympathetic view of the former than the latter. People in the first instance are seen as 'victims'; those in the second, as 'guilty'. It was also shown to be the case that people who are engaged on issues of poverty in the First World become active about the subject in the Third World—but not the reverse.

5.   It seems to me that this suggests a pattern for Christian witness: Those who wish to 'be concerned' focus their attention on poverty in the sphere which is most removed from themselves; they then are able to offer supports of remedies that have little or no implication for their own lifestyle. It is a case of people who demonstrate Fowler's Stage 4 of development evolving a focus which suggests that they exercise

to tackle the issues at all. The liberal Church, on the other hand, attempts to alter the economic system through a process of moral preaching without changing the prevailing rules of the game.[6] Sermons on socio-economic morality are just right: they are sufficiently generalized to obviate programmes for action, but allow us to feel concerned.[7] Unfortunately, they cannot take the place of consistent and effective policy. Our third defence is in some respects the most interesting and, given the title of this conference, perhaps the most relevant. We attempt to convert the world—economic systems in their 'secular context'—without converting ourselves. We operate on a sheep-shepherd-sheepfold model based on a misreading of John 10.[8] We act as though the sheepfold is the place to enter, to be safe, to be separate, and as though this segregation and isolation is a sacred space from which we only dash out to collect up others to drag in and to stay inside. The obligations of the sacred space are different from and have little consequence for activity outside the space. The chief object is to stay (at least to retreat) inside, rather than seriously to alter the structures of the outside on the basis of the inside's energy or to take any of the energy and aspects of life from the outside to the inside. But the metaphor says that Jesus is the gate—the connecting place, not the bar between spaces; the pasture is on the outside; liberation and salvation are free passage between the two: we are called to go redeemingly in and out, in and out.

The twentieth-century Church erects these defences through a variable process of splitting, the long recognized technique for maintaining resistance to change, challenge and growth. Splitting is a technique to which the tendency in modern society for compartmentalism has particularly conditioned us. Within the ministry and organized life of the Church, we operate it institutionally, congregationally and individually.

Institutionally, we split off socio-economic issues into specialist forms of ministry or particular foci which keep us as the practising Church (in hierarchy and as gathered congregations) at one remove from the issues: to wit, industrial mission. Working externally, as though the 'outside world' has little connection with the Church, we ally ourselves with the

---

the reflection and responsibility of that characterizes people in Stage 4 (Fowler, *Faith Developer*, pp. 68ff.).

6. 'Third Ways and Middle Axioms', in J.L. Segundo, *The Liberation of Theology* (Maryknoll, NY: Orbis, 1985), pp. 92-93.

7. Hull, *What Prevents Christian Adults from Learning?*, pp. 132-33.

8. Hull, *What Prevents Christian Adults from Learning?*, pp. 66-67, 129-30.

best, most creative, apparently charitable strands of the existing economic system (which continues to aggregate wealth and power) and call that witness for the kingdom.[9]

Splitting functions at the level of gathered congregations, too, where the nuts and bolts of building Christian witness is done.[10] In order to highlight the connections with Brueggemann's analysis of prophecy, I want to focus on the role of tradition, and particularly the Bible, as it supports splitting in the formation of Christian witness. These days, certainly in the Anglican tradition, Christian congregations are instructed chiefly though the preaching office (including the reading of scripture) of Sunday worship. The scriptures and Christian tradition from the post-biblical age are replete with teachings on the requirements for economic justice and the liberation of the poor as a salvation prerequisite. But Christian congregations are consistently protected from that teaching. They are given very little instruction in Church and tradition history; less of biblical history. They are not equipped or encouraged to reflect critically on scripture or tradition and have no learning experience concerning the nature of biblical composition, the sociology of the Bible, or doctrines of inspiration. Sermons are based in the generalizations of doctrine (e.g., incarnation, creation, trinity) which are all too readily 'spiritualized' and emptied of material content and easily collapsed to individual issues of personal piety and morality. This myopia is aided and abetted in Anglicanism by the increased focus on the Eucharist. Much of the biblical teaching which is embedded in the God of history and attested in specific ethical teaching, the story of covenant faithfulness or failure, is in the Old Testament. Few Christians are ever exposed to it, in church or out (this is certainly true of the Church of England). The Gospels are denuded of their political and economic dimension in favour of their 'spiritual content' (consider Matthew's sermon on the mount) and are read to the exclusion of the Old Testament. Most so-called ethical teaching is offered on the basis of Paul and the epistles rather than

---

9.   It seems to me that one of the resolutions of the 1994 IMA Conference in Iona is an example of this tendency:

> The conference recommends that the IMA, in view of the contracting resources available to industrial mission and a continuing strong concern for the poor and the marginalised, should maintain and use to the full our contacts with the major institutions of wealth creation, in the cause of justice and wholeness for our society.

10.   Hull, *What Prevents Christian Adults from Learning?*, ch. 2, 'The Education of the Ideological Community', pp. 45-88.

the gospels, and Paul (at least as rendered) is virtually devoid of political and economic consciousness—except as he teaches to protect the institutions that were threatened by and threatening to Christians. Even when Christians are exposed directly to scripture, they certainly are not encouraged to explore, question or apply it. They are given no opportunities to set the lives and lessons of which it speaks against their own lives, as if God is active in either. So, we stay snug with concerns about the collapse of marriage and the family, without having to bother about the economic forces that mediate against both and fracture all sorts of community.[11]

Perhaps the saddest splitting is that which occurs in the lives of ministers (pastors and priests, as well as lay professional).[12] A poignant example is the story of industrial missioners: Industrial Mission practitioners are generally good at social and economic analysis. They frequently articulate (or used to articulate) alternative futures for the economy; sometimes they devise programmes to achieve an alternative (even if partial) and carry them out at least within limited spheres. The work of missioners arises from convictions of faith, is based in and informed by theology, although often more fully in doctrinal terms (the more theoretical, rationalized and generalized discipline) than in spiritual terms. But all too often and in a variety of ways, their working lives (and sometimes their interior lives) are isolated, not to say severed, from the institutional Church. Hence, the expertise and vision of fifty years of Industrial Mission has made very little impact on and is very little valued by the Church as 'church'. Missioners work full-time 'in the secular structures', so they have no parochial responsibilities. Sometimes when a part-time missioner has care of a congregation or parish, he or she is able to carry very little of Industrial Mission into the parochial tasks. All too often, missioners feel altogether alienated or marginalized (exiled!) from the institution—from its structures, from its gathered worship and community, from its witness and concerns. Above all, missioners do far

---

11. *The Gospel, the Poor and the Churches*, section 3.

12. *The Gospel, the Poor and the Churches*. The clergy tended to give poverty a higher priority in the life of the Church than did the laity. No clergy were in groups that blamed or were unsympathetic to the poor; the laity more commonly blamed the poor. Clergy more commonly adopted a political stance to the issues than did the laity. *Nonetheless*, among the clergy who were committed to work for justice for the economically marginalized, some split this concern off from the care for their flocks and were concerned 'not to burden' their congregations with these issues.

too little adult education/formation within the Christian community that is specifically gathered as Church. This is through pressure of other work, because the structures are not in place to allow it, or because individual churches do not want it or recognise the issues of Industrial Mission as having any thing to do with faith; and lastly, perhaps, because we are so disenchanted with or frustrated by 'Church' that we can not be bothered. Like the ministers of the Christian Aid survey, I suspect that missionaries do the work we do to justify our faith commitments and collude with the institutional marginalization in an attempt to keep a modicum of comfort in our contact with and experience of 'Church'. But the cost is very high. We are cut off from the energy and affirmation of the faith community, exhausted and divided in ourselves.

It is clear to me that Industrial Mission has always had a prophetic desire: We work to transform economic systems that fail equitably to distribute wealth and power. We consistently fail to make a significant impact, however, because we do not effectively articulate the function of prophecy. The first order task of prophecy is always to convert and to transform the faithful group; the second order, to transform the work. I suggest that Industrial Mission needs to shift its focus from the second order to the first order task; that it should focus much more on its work on the church community and that its role within that community is best fulfilled through adult education. Christian education that is able to be truly prophetic would have four characteristics: (1) It should be biblically based. (2) It should use experiential and participatory methods. (3) It should always invite people to do the necessary socio-economic and political analysis and to knit the contemporary analysis with parallel situations in biblical (and Church) history. (4) It should develop and make regular use of teaching techniques which enable people to imagine achievable socio-economic alternatives (micro and macro) and devise programmes for action which implement them.

1. *Biblical tradition:* There are several reasons why prophetic education needs roots in the Bible, not least for the treatment of current faith-backed socio-economic learning. The first is that it provides a common ground for shared history, commitment and language. In my experience, one of the first tasks in working with church people on economic issues is to demonstrate to them that the agenda for which the Church has given me some responsibility is common to the agenda of gathered congregations. Work with scripture achieves that nexus. It further allows

me to invite people to reflect on issues without preaching at them, thus without inviting simplistic confrontation and denial.[13] A second reason is that the Bible is the repository of the events and revelation of the God who acts in human history and in partnership with people. In the face of this reality, it is more difficult for church people to argue that events of contemporary social systems are not the realm of revelation and salvation. Thirdly, there is a stratum of the Bible that is significant for salvation and that has been lost us: the agenda of God and God's people with the poor. We need to retrieve that agenda so that it can call us to conversion; when it is retrieved, work on contemporary issues for economic justice can proceed more easily.[14] Fourthly, work with scripture, including its history, composition and criticism, empowers the people of God to take their rightful place as theologians: commitment for covenant action grows where people are personally and consciously engaged in the activity of salvation and creation. Finally, the uncovered variety, plurality and complexity of the biblical record is a primary means to assist us to reflect on the plurality of the modern age in a constructive, liberating way: Christianity is a many-sided faith. With this awareness, we can claim the possibility for relatedness, as opposed to disjunction, that is present to us in pluralism and secularism.[15]

2. *Experiential and participatory methods* allow people to use the material of their own lives as the ground of study and discovery. The telling of our stories is the appropriate tool of theology.[16] When the narratives of faith history (the people and stories of scripture) meet the narratives of our own lives, we are at the horizon of God's dialogue with the community of faith—it is the place where the past of God with us meets the present of God with us. The practice of comparative biography encourages people to become aware of the evolution of their own belief system; further, it is in hearing about others' lives and beliefs that we become truly aware of our own.[17] Secondly, when people use

13. Hull, *What Prevents Christian Adults from Learning?*, pp. 103-111.

14. Any number of liberation theology commentaries is useful. W. Brueggemann, *Abiding Astonishment* (Literary Currents in Biblical Interpretation; Louisville: Westminster Press, 1991) is also very interesting in this respect.

15. Hull, *What Prevents Christian Adults from Learning?*, p. 118 and pp. 79-82.

16. There is a variety of texts on narrative and theology. M. Goldberg, *Theology and Narrative* (Philadelphia: Trinity Press International, 1991) and G.A. Lindbeck, *The Nature of Doctrine* (London: SPCK, 1984) are two that I have found helpful.

17. Hull, *What Prevents Christian Adults from Learning?*, p. 11

their own stories or enter into processes which insert them into the stories of others, they actively participate in actions and events, even if only in a limited way. It is an educational axiom that people learn and are changed by what they experience rather than by what they are told,[18] and prophetic education seeks to change us. Thirdly, participatory methods help to overcome the resistance to learning which arises in adults from an unconscious self-interest. They constitute a method which places what people believe to be true alongside a different reality that claims validity.[19] The result is the state of 'cognitive dissonance', which is a powerful ground for learning and change. Precisely because the methods build powerful spaces, however, educational occasions which make use of such methods must be carefully prepared and people engaged in them must be adequately supported.[20] Finally, participatory methods offer people a learning ground; they do not simply deliver information. The result is that people who participate are also delivered the responsibility for their own judgment, change and growth.

3. *Socio-economic and political analysis.* The understanding of current structures, is necessary if people are to identify their place in them; people must locate themselves in their own systems if they wish to have any hope of changing them. Using methods that encourage and support analysis is no easy task. In the first place, analysis results in a double edged conviction: on the one hand, we see ourselves implicated in unjust systems and are invited to judgment; on the other, we are liberated from the conspiracy of secrecy and accumulated power which makes it easy for us to believe that 'things are the way they are because they must be the way they are'. The energy for change and the hope for an alternative future, however, comes precisely from such conviction. When we understand how the system works, we will also discover what makes it change and where we, as the people we are, have purchase for change on the system.

4. *Facilitating socio-economic alternatives.* Finally, when we have come to know our own stories; when we have learned to set our history against the biblical record of the God who is always with us in events;

18. C.E. Reagan and D. Stewart (eds.), *The Philosophy of Paul Ricoeur* (Boston: Beacon Press, 1979), especially chs. 15 and 16.

19. Hull, *What Prevents Christian Adults from Learning?*, pp. 96 and 102.

20. Hull, *What Prevents Christian Adults from Learning?*, pp. 102-11.

then we will have the ability to descry the events of God's salvation in the affairs of our world. Prophetic action arises from an education that enables us to *imagine achievable alternatives* to dominant socio-economic policy and *to devise programmes for action which implement them.* Processes which implement models such as personal construct theory[21] allow learners to play with new ideas and to entertain them without any threat of heavy commitment. When these ideas are rooted in experience and validated by data, they can be rendered as concrete and delimited strategies for change. Finite strategies for change which are informed by systemic analysis become the building blocks for a converted existence— which is otherwise known as the kingdom of God.

Brueggemann calls the operation of prophecy, as it can be articulated in a programme of education such as I have described, *the practice of poetry.*[22] Rooted in an analysis of Jeremiah's language, Brueggemann identifies these characteristics of prophets as poets: (1) They have no advice to give to people but only want to encourage people to see life differently, to re-vision. In place of coercion, they practice stimulation, surprise, hint and nuance. (2) Their language is porous: it is not exhausted in a first hearing; it leaves things open and ambiguous, available for further reflection. Prophets do not pretend to know the future; they offer the present as shockingly open and ambiguous ground from which various futures may emerge. Their images neither compel nor instruct: they only push listeners to think further about the world and our posture within it. (3) They use porous language because it leaves the poetry—the possible constructions of past into future—open for the experience of the listener. It is a language that requires rich metaphors that are open and polyvalent. Such language prevents the images of the prophet from being slotted into already existing categories which the listener can simply reject, resist and argue against. It intends to shatter and to violate the categories with which the listener operates.

Hull describes the use of construct theory and cognitive conflict in Christian adult education as the practice of *loose construing.*[23] These techniques invite learners to cross the boundaries and strata of the systems and pluralities in which they operate. They assist us to set the issues of our contemporary, secular existence against the living reality of our

21. Hull, *What Prevents Christian Adults from Learning?*
22. Brueggemann, *Hopeful Imagination*, pp. 23-25
23. Hull, *What Prevents Christian Adults from Learning?*, pp. 101-102.

historical faith in order to discern God's salvation and creation in the making—and to be partners in the liberation of the gospel for our world. If industrial missioners can learn the necessary educational skills, employ their existing skills in analysis and economic understanding, and powerfully address the people of God in first order of prophecy; then the people of God can undertake the second level of prophecy which is their task: The conversion, in community, of the world.

Such a ministry will be both the practice of poetry and the function of loose construing. It will be concerned, as was the ministry of Jeremiah, at least as much with the *invitation to imagination* as it is with the *practice of ethics*.[24] It will protect industrial missioners and the people with whom we work from the abuses of power which frequently accompany ministry in various forms today: 'Teachers' in this kind of activity are also learners. They do not possess all the knowledge, nor can they dictate the conclusions of the learning experience. Both educators and 'learners' are empowered to make a community journey. Such ministers are not 'in control', and all parties are thus more open to the in-breaking of God. The practice of such a ministry grows from a vocation that is vulnerable, wild, dangerous and mysterious; it is the only kind of ministry that is appropriate to the ground of the holy.

24. Hull, *What Prevents Christian Adults from Learning?*, p. 25.

MISSION AND ECONOMY: CULTURE, VALUE AND CREATION

Rachel Jenkins

In this paper, there are three sections. The first is an analysis of the working situation that is prevalent in contemporary Britain. The second covers some of the dilemmas which people face as they work in this kind of setting; the third section discusses what kind of mission may emerge. The paper raises more questions than it answers, for which I make no apology. Our failure to look carefully at the realities around us, or to be bounced into finding solutions with immediate effect, are weaknesses to which it is all too easy to succumb in the present climate, for reasons which will emerge in the first section.

What Are the Dominant Principles at Work in Contemporary Britain?

It is important to say that the answer to the question given here is based on research in the public as well as the private sector. Your own situation may differ from this in emphasis, it may be radically different, or you may find many similarities.

The Market Is Seen as the Most Important Regulator of Policy

Markets consist of those who supply and those who demand—economic terms which mean that there are sellers and buyers for every commodity. Because there is competition between all those who sell and between all those who buy, the price of each commodity is expected to reach a 'realistic' or competitive level. On the basis of this belief and commitment, we have seen our National Health Service reorganized into a kind of market (but not one with open competition).[1] We have also seen schools marketing themselves, producing glossy leaflets extolling their facilities and philosophies. There is much to be said for public institutions engaging

---

1. Professor Chris Ham of the Health Service Management Centre at the University of Birmingham, quoted in *The Guardian*, 19 January 1994.

in discussions about the nature of their work, but certain anxieties about the cost of such exercises and the benefits of competition with other schools remain.

The Commitment to Competitiveness Is Driven by Short Terms Goals and Gains
Much of the thinking around the marketing of goods and services is extremely short term. Results are looked for in the current or next financial year. Few discussions about policy are looking even five years ahead let alone into the next century. At certain levels managers in the National Health Service and in some high street banks are engaged on one year contracts. They are expected to reach certain levels of efficiency or productivity. Failure to do so will mean they are not re-employed. How can long term policies be developed under these circumstances? In business enterprises there is a tendency to talk about outcomes, but to avoid the debate about rationale, or the impact of outcomes on employees, the local community, the environment, or the long-term effects on the organization itself.[2] How many Church of England dioceses are worrying about balancing the books, without asking questions about the kind of church they want to promote for the coming century?

The Demands on Workers at All Levels Are Based on Total Efficiency and Productivity
In some settings this means that there is little or no time for discussions about policies, or the development of good staff relations. Policy development is often centralized, and local units are simply expected to development instructions. Workers who have poor attendance records, for whatever reasons, are often the target of redundancy policies, as experience in one of the high street banks has shown.

In the name of efficiency, in a company providing public services, leave patterns have been rescheduled, to make the incidence equal throughout the year, without taking into account the known effect of the weather on the variations in repair work. Workers in the field have to account for every minute spent—there is a growing sense that employers do not trust their employees. At the same time, employees are often expected to be responsible for customer relations and to take initiatives well beyond their job descriptions. (If you are familiar with the advertisements for

---

2.   Michael Black (Vice-President of the Management Consultancy CSC index) quoted in *The Observer*, 30 January 1994).

Marriott hotels, you will know that this is called in certain circles 'staff empowerment'.) Great loyalty is expected from employees, but they rarely experience a sense that their employers are loyal to them.

Finally the demand for productivity lays great emphasis on what can be measured, and very little on the unmeasurable aspects of the job. The exam results are made the measure of a school's success without taking into account the background of its pupils or the level of resources which the school has to offer. The number of patients treated in a hospital is important, although the negative experiences of being a day patient for surgery is ignored because the lack of community nursing services is the responsibility of another Trust.

Professional Experience Is Being Devalued

Attacks have been made on professional groups as self-seeking and not under public control. One of the effects of these attacks has been to undermine the value of professional opinions. If the teachers develop rational arguments about the changes in the education system, they are often dismissed as being expressions of self-interest. In November 1993 the former chief scientist at the Department of Health spoke of the government's pattern of 'brushing aside the expertise of doctors and other health professionals and boosting inexperienced managers'.[3]

Rejection of the Value of Objective Knowledge

There is worrying evidence that carefully developed research is set aside if it does not fit with what the commissioning organization expected. Research into the National Curriculum has been conducted on terms dictated by the Department for Education which prevented researchers from discussing their work with other academics. At least one senior academic has had work substantially rewritten by civil servants, but cannot comment because of the contract under which the research has been conducted.[4]

What Kind of Dilemmas Do People Face?

Effects of The Market

As the radical changes in the National Health Service were proposed, and later implemented, many staff found themselves ill at ease with the

3. Dr Peter Woodford quoted in *The Guardian*, 31 January 1994.
4. Barry Hugill in *The Observer*, 23 January 1994.

philosophy which they represented. Specialist departments were aware that the service which they provided would no longer be available on a needs basis, but on the basis of which part of the institution could pay for their work. Professionals who had a lifelong commitment to the principles of a *national* health service now found themselves working in a service which was anything but national, and which tended to provide services to those sections which could best afford their work. Did this matter? Could they simply accept that times were changing, and that the nature of their work was not substantially altered? The main change they had to accept was the way in which their work was delivered or distributed. Did the underlying values matter, if the work could proceed in much the same way?

Bank staff working to make profit levels increase begin to offer the most profitable service to their customers rather than the most appropriate. If you are a senior person with responsibility for junior staff, including their training, and if you believe that your work is to find the most appropriate service for all customers, how do you reconcile your principles with the instructions which are being issued?

In both these cases I am referring to people who are not in a position to affect the process by which policies are developed.

Short Term Goals and Gains, Efficiency and Productivity

Where managers on short contracts are responsible for the productivity of workers under them, there is tremendous pressure to maintain and increase productivity. Among the banking sector, there has been talk of aiming for increasing efficiency 10% one year, followed by 8%, followed by 5%. How can this be possible? If one branch or sector is failing to reach its targets, the prescribed procedure is to cut costs, usually by making staff redundant. A senior manager and one of his sector managers belong to the same parish. The senior manager says he has to leave his Christianity behind every time he goes to work. He is concerned that the sector manager is not reaching the productivity required. Since the senior manager is on a one year contract he rightly sees that one or other of them will lose employment.

Where a midwife spends over an hour completing the seven different forms relating to a normal hospital delivery, she may enable the unit to claim the funds on which it depends, but she is spending less time with the women who are her professional responsibility.

A new term is being used in management 'the intensification of work'. It refers to the increasing work burdens which people in employment are carrying. Recent reports referred to the high rate of early retirement among head teachers. Informants in the private sector tell me that in their work places they see people at all levels working up to 25% more than 8–10 years ago. With this kind of pressure, people are afraid of taking time off, because of the long term effects this will have on their own work load and on their colleagues. Equally disturbing is the tendency for employers to look with disapproval on staff who take time off sick. Some redundancies in the banking services have been determined by attendance records.

At a recent international conference, we regretted the lack of people from the former centrally planned economies. We were told by our contacts in Poland that people are reluctant to take time off work. Their jobs are so much under pressure that people were not taking their full holiday entitlement.

The Devaluing of Professional Experience and the Rejection of Objective knowledge

There are many examples where professional expertise and careful research have been rejected on the grounds of dogma: the alteration to the content and process of the national music curriculum by civil servants and politicians; and the ignoring of the research by the probation officer's association, NACRO and the Howard League for penal reform on the inappropriateness of some forms of sentencing. Among hospital social workers, their professional expertise to identify the needs of the client is now subsidiary to the task of discovering what the client can afford; and what the service can afford to provide.

In Conclusion

People are faced not with one dilemma but with many. The responsibilities they carry in their work have changed substantially leaving their original skills diminished.

Competitive management policies are undermining, if not destroying the professional co-operation in which much of our public service work depends. A recent article in *The Guardian* argued that clinical standards will fall because short term objectives will lead to a diminishing sense of wider responsibility.[5]

Employees who are concerned about the developments in their workplace, or the wider organizations, do not easily find ways of expressing

5. *The Guardian*, 1 August 1994.

their concern which will be heard and acted upon. Trades union activities have been curtailed, and contact with the press runs the risk of suspension or dismissal (see the case of Graham Pink, and others who have publicly criticised health service policies). In general, people who draw attention to failures of public policy or to illegal practices receive harsh treatment in Britain.[6]

In summary, women and men are in work settings where the practices are changing, where the purpose of their organization has been radically changed, and where their own values and principles are undermined or contradicted by the organization which employs them. Many are so uncomfortable they would like to move, but in the present economic climate few opportunities are available. Moreover, the patterns discussed here are pervasive in the public, private and voluntary sectors, so a change of job may not mean a more acceptable context.

What Kind of Mission May Emerge?
The challenge of continuing to work in these difficult settings requires serious theological consideration. The mission I see emerging comes from the people who are in these settings. It is not a mission which 'the Church' (in whatever forms) devises for them.

It is a mission of profound theological reflection. There are no easy, comforting messages from the confusions which we face. No-one can seriously assert that all 'is for the best' or piously advise that all should be left in God's hands. Those hands do not feel very safe.

The mission that emerges asks difficult and disturbing questions. It is a mission which recognizes the danger and risks which people face, and gives them permission to articulate their fears and their doubts as a legitimate form of theological reflection. Reflecting on their own needs to compromise, a group of managers asked 'Is God ever compromised?' It felt a dangerous place to be—but the right question to ask and struggle with. We have no clear answer, but need to go on working with whatever insights we discover.

The mission that emerges acknowledges the pain that people experience, and does not pretend that it will be easily cured. Like arthritis it is always there with ability to restrict our movements, sometimes more acute and obvious than at others. It is a mission that is not afraid to name what is wrong, but it also tries to act as creatively as possible within the

6. M. Winfield, *Minding Your Own Business: Self Regulation and Whistle Blowing in the British Companies*, 1990 Social Audit.

surrounding limitations. It is a mission which accepts the necessity of compromise, without constantly berating those who cannot avoid compromise. It is a mission which continues to believe that it is possible to live by alternative values, not as a weak optimism, but as a driving belief, however difficult it is to maintain.

For texts by theologians see:

W. Brueggemann, *The Prophetic Imagination* (Philadelphia: Fortress Press, 1978).
R. Fung, *The Isaiah Vision: An Ecumenical Strategy for Congregational Evangelism* (Geneva: WCC, 1992).
S.D. Welch, *A Feminist Ethic of Risk* (Philadelphia: Fortress Press, 1990).

THEOLOGICAL AUDIT—INTERPRETED AND APPLIED THEOLOGY: A METHOD OF PAIRED EXAMINATION OF OUR OWN DISCIPLESHIP IN THE SPECIFIC AREAS OF INDIVIDUAL OCCUPATION

Peter Challen

> Something must be done to bridge the gulf between scholars' robust and powerful insights and the more anaemic stuff often offered to the person-in-the-pew. It is commonly said that the latter cannot take theology, but this is patronising slander; when presented in suitable form and terms the material is welcomed hungrily.

Thus speaks Roger Dowley,[1] who read 40 works of biblical scholarship and then distilled important communal themes that he, an ardent evangelical, saw for the first time throbbing through the stories of those who searched for meaning and for public accountability in the human condition.

After 15 years, my practice of 'theological auditing' ranges from the gentle probing of discipleship at work to the severe and willing reappraisal of professional responsibilities. Its main characteristics as a tool are flexibility, expandability and its range of application. It requires the drawing together of both pastoral trust and prophetic opportunities, to evoke what might be from what is. It is a means of 'doing theology' on the job, in the economy, as a contribution to the common good. It claims that the field of exploration is a faith that God reigns in all of life, even if it is not known (in advance) how. We can only search so as to enhance our commitment to make the poetic creeds a practical way to walk in. 'Theological auditing' calls upon the conviction that the Christian influence on our lives lies in our energized memories and our knowledge of being summoned by radical hope.

Its 'audit' foundation lies in the OED definition, 'a searching exami-

---

1. Personal letter to the author. See Dowley's book *Towards the Recovery of a Lost Bequest: A Layman's Work Notes on the Biblical Pattern for a Just Commentary* (London: Scripture Union, n.d).

nation (especially the day of judgment)', which makes possible a good humoured but valid claim to a relationship between faithfulness and accountability. Its 'theological' foundation lies in the responsibility of the *Laos*, ordained or not, as 'jobbing theologians' to explore their discipleship in all the manifestations, complexities and knock-on effects over time and space, of their actions and decisions. First consider some examples:

1. A Health and Safety Officer identified in a theological audit the disturbing sense of being forced to be a regulator for the government. After her audit, her re-evaluated discipleship within her professional capacity led to a recognition of the need to be an enabler for the intrinsic worth of health and safety in each workplace she visited. This realization gave her the courage to leave the relative security of the civil service and slowly, even painfully, to earn the authentic status of an independent consultant. After two years in the wilderness her consultancy now flourishes; and levels of health and safety rise significantly.

2. A quarterly forum and a correspondence network on 'Accountancy with Theological Resonance', now numbers 80 financial professionals and amateurs, who together probe the demands of accounting for sustainability.

3. Twenty persons each year, in training for ordination to stipendiary or non-stipendiary ministry, submit themselves to a theological audit in the third year with painful but exhilarating effect.

4. Individuals work with South London Industrial Mission chaplains, at levels appropriate to the associates' courage and ability to stretch and translate their theological perceptions, on designing their own theological audit from several available models.

The process of theological auditing has proved effective with several bodies and with more than 700 individuals ready to probe their discipleship and apply new insights to specific situations.

Theological auditing is a one-to-one engagement. To be effective it requires six dedicated hours spread over whatever period is agreed. It is a highly flexible tool that relates specific situations to a comprehensive faith in life. It is a means by which an organization can be introduced to applied and practical theology. It is a way by which individuals can deepen and extend their discipleship. It is a process that elides threshold counselling, good communications and critique of the enterprise in society with 'doing theology'.

It proceeds through these 8 stages:[2]

1. The person voluntarily submitting to audit makes a detailed identification of their work's general context and their own specific 'text' within it. Thus we get a real locale, that can now begin be related to instinctive human wisdom and/or revelation revisited. An opportunity is opened up to challenge perspective, assumptions and conventions rarely brought under the eye of faith.

2. In this process the auditor gives true 'amateur' attention—that is the concentrated attention of someone who loves the subject for its own intrinsic value and is motivated to hear the details of both opportunity and dilemma within it. The playing back of what is seen and heard begins to widen the awareness of the auditee.

3. Next we look at the auditee's comprehension of his or her faith tradition and religious perspective on life. This examines where the person already is in the understanding and application of a lively faith. It usually reveals selective understanding and even elements of self-justification by that partial faith.

4. Auditor and auditee then work to extend the comprehension of the biblical faith in a postmodern society. This is the process of identifying a wide, global, open context within which great themes of revelation are revisited; themes of instinctive human wisdom; of some aspects of natural law; and of whatever sources of perspective are available to the pair with all their network of connection and experience. Themes that emerge from memory or as freshly recognized insights buried in ancient recitations, often at first perplex the auditee, but soon stir him or her to intriguing new aspects of discipleship. This recovery of the lost bequest of a covenant with all the earth, 'everything under the rainbow', includes such communal

2.   Examples of some stages in the 'theological audit' process are included at the end of the paper.

imperatives as: creation (the ecology portfolio); heritage (wisdom and gifts with which we are endowed); jubilee (regular restructuring for justice); shalom (an all-pervading peace with justice); covenant (to be contrasted with our present contract culture); kingdom (the global ethic and economy of total common good); eternity (the biblical suggestion of much that 'sustainablity' now includes and requires of our trusteeship); calling/vocation (servant of that public good in all circumstances); blessing (gift of grace as a precondition of trusteeship and ownership); torah (an ordering of the sustainable global community in the making, such as sets a total context for our local codes and ethical behaviour). This immense and often neglected bequest of energized memories summons us to radical economic hope. It sets the scene for the detail of the localized and specific theological audit.

5. Now, with the groundwork prepared, the audit discipline itself proceeds in detail. The auditee is asked to identify some test themes that have come to her or him afresh or even for the first time. These are the themes that regularly reappear when humans search for meaning in the structures of our society. They restore the communal aspect of the public accountability that we all hold as children of God.

6. With these particular test themes detailed, examination is then made and affirmed in pursuit, or fulfilment, of the chosen themes. Very often some aspects of the theme are already known and quietly enacted, but, because of lack of affirmation or recognition by others, little effort is made to improve the contribution or even identify it. This affirmation is essential to the creation of trust that the audit is a very serious and attentive appraisal. It makes the creeds a way to walk in, a way to work in, a contribution to public accountability.

7. On the basis of the trust generated by genuine affirmation, it is then possible to look in detail at the blockages before, or constraints upon, the development of these important themes of human response to the purposes of God. These preventative forces, assumptions or conventions are rigorously detailed. They are the enemies of justice and peace set in the integrity of creation, that we must share in defeating. Individual contribution is identified as having humble but genuine significance.

As one auditee expressed it: 'Tomorrow does not lie in tomorrow, but in every butterfly that weathers today's storms; and in the synergy of their contributions to the future patterns of our days'.

8.   In the light of a now far better understanding of the difficulties that stand in our way the final part of the audit is to imagine the creative ways of circumnavigating, overriding or breaking down the blockages that lie before us. This involves the setting of some limited but responsible targets, of planning for the evaluation of our attempt to reach them, and of the regular resetting of targets as we work out our discipleship in an ever dynamic situation, year on year.

Theological audits have changed patterns of individuals' work and teams' contributions in many places where faith is not readily accepted as having pertinence: in accounting; in contracts and covenants; in perceptions of wealth; in training; in redeploying; in brokerage; in information technology; even in map making; in the introduction of sustainability; in career changes; in absorbing patterns of new economics...and so on, and so forth.

Theological audit increases the possibility of bringing faithfulness into all the underlined aspects of this so called 'Brisbane Statement':

> The proclamation of Jesus Christ as the crucified and risen Lord and the confession that Jesus Christ is Lord have both an *intimate* and *cosmic* implication. We cannot confess Jesus Christ is Lord without serious consequences for the ordering of *political* and *economic relationships* and the harmony in which *humankind* lives as *a part of the whole creation*. (Brisbane: Anglican Mission Agencies, 1986.)

Christians are prone to acknowledge this fine statement and ignore its challenge. They approve it and then fail to apply the reigning of God to the underlined applications beyond that which is here called the 'intimate'. All the other applications are personal too, though not intimate. The economic, the political, and the relationships of humankind to the created environment in which we are set are conveniently, or conventionally, forgotten. But they are the personal concern of all, and surprisingly often an element of our personal responsibility. This forgetting, theological auditing makes less likely.

Theological Audit Matrix

Two foundations there are which bear upon public societies. The one a natural inclination whereby all desire sociable life and fellowship; the other an order...agreed upon...touching the manner of their union in living together.[3]

Mode of Living Story/Structure	Affirmed in my Occupations	Negated by Mind Sets & Obstacles	Restored by my Initiatives
Creation: Integrity & Sustainability			
Covenant & Contract			
Shalom & Torah			
Sabbath, Release & Jubilee			
Wealth, Health, Salvation & Work			
Justice: Personal, Structured & Global			
Prophetic Imagination. Education/Training/ Grief & Energising			
Awe, Glory, Worthship & Liturgy			
Trinity/Planning Doing & Evaluating			
Servanthood			

And
    many
        more
           themes
              and modes
                of your own choosing
                    But !!! tackle the tougher and more unusual themes.

3.   Hooker, 'Ecclesiastical Polity'.

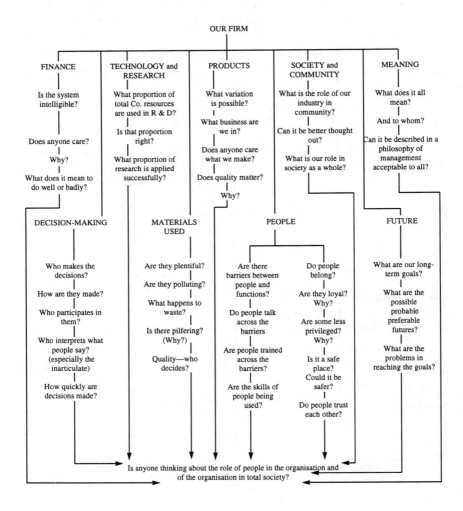

URBAN REGENERATION INITIATIVES AND THE CHURCHES

Hilary Russell

Introduction

The urban face of Britain has been transformed over the past quarter of a century. This period has seen the erosion of many traditional industries. Cities have lost both people and jobs. Their economic and fiscal base has declined. Their physical environments have deteriorated. They have experienced a concentration of socially and economically vulnerable groups. But while economic and social problems have increased, the autonomy and capacity of cities to address them has declined. This paper looks at:

Policy trends over the past twenty five years. The paper traces the move away from the welfare-based approach to urban problems of the 1960s to a greater emphasis on economic regeneration. It identifies changing government attitudes towards the involvement of local authorities and the private sector in the planning and delivery of regeneration.

The principles of current policy as exemplified in City Challenge. City Challenge was the government's flagship urban regeneration initiative of the early 1990s. It exemplifies a cross-sectoral, partnership-based approach which, even though this initiative may not be renewed, has wider lessons.

The role of churches in regeneration partnerships. Churches have an opportunity to participate in regeneration initiatives as members of the community and voluntary sector. The paper looks at what they may bring to a partnership table. It also poses the questions which such involvement might raise for churches themselves about their culture, organization and priorities.

A Moving Spotlight on Inner Cities

Urban policy as an explicit strand of public policy was only introduced in 1968. Since then, it has undergone various re-incarnations. In the early decades after 1945, governments relied on the welfare state and the planning system to meet the needs of both individuals and cities. In the 1960s, mounting evidence of urban poverty plus some unease about race relations led the Labour government to introduce a new policy, managed by the Home Office, targeted specifically at inner cities. The programme was basically a welfare-based response to urban social problems.

Community Development Projects (CDPs) provided accounts of this early experience and its lessons about the nature and causes of decline in their areas. They provided the essential message subsequently incorporated in the 1977 White Paper, *Policy for the Inner Cities*, which gave the first coherent diagnosis of inner city problems. It indicated that the reason for these concentrations of deprivation was not individual failings, but the decline or collapse of the economic activity on which people had depended for their livelihood, accompanied by selective population loss. The aims of government policy therefore widened beyond alleviating social problems to strengthening local economies, improving the physical fabric and securing a better balance between inner areas and the wider city region. Responsibility was transferred to the DoE. The policy was delivered through Inner City Partnerships, intended to link central and local government, the private sector and community groups.

The White Paper contained 'the first step along the road to regeneration by enterprise'.[1] Its diagnosis of what was wrong and prescription of what needed to be done also appealed to the incoming Conservative government of 1979. But the new administration differed radically in its policy for pursuing these goals. For Labour, public expenditure was seen as key to the exercise. Local government was still regarded as a main agent in urban regeneration. With the change of government, the new response to urban decline was private sector led urban entrepreneurialism; a move from 'public provision to private enterprise'.[2] Policy instruments were developed with the objectives of making investment in certain

---

1.　N. Deakin and J. Edwards, *The Enterprise Culture and the Inner City* (London: Routledge, 1993), p. 20.

2.　Deakin and Edwards, *The Enterprise Culture*, heading to ch. 2.

areas more attractive, through such measures as relaxing planning regulations, making land available, giving exemptions from taxes or rates and levering in private money.

With the dissolution of a bipartisan approach nationally came a clash of agendas between central government and the Labour administrations in many cities who were still convinced that only the public sector was capable of 'staunching the haemorrhaging caused by private sector disinvestment'.[3] This period also saw, therefore, a growth in local government intervention in economic development, covering such activities as physical redevelopment, enterprise development, co-operative and community development, promotional policies and municipal interventions in the labour market. But the impact of this activity was limited because local authorities' resources were so severely restricted.

The government's move to enlist the private sector as the key driver of regeneration was part of a bigger strategy to redistribute political power. It was determined to reduce the power of local authorities and break their control as monopoly suppliers of public services. In urban finance, increasingly complex grant mechanisms were created intended to curb cities' revenue and capital spending. Government substantially reduced the level of resources provided to cities and restricted their ability to raise their own resources or spend those they had. There was an increasing imbalance between the 'icing' in the form of Urban Programme funds and a disappearing 'cake' in terms of main programmes. Many urban services were privatized or deregulated either by the enforced sale of city assets or by opening the way for private companies to supply local services. The overall effect has been to reduce the coherence of the financial system and make it increasingly difficult for cities to plan or control their environment and deliver high quality services.

The DoE report, *Assessing the Impact of Urban Policy*, reviewed the whole package of Action for Cities policy instruments. It tried to measure changes in the conditions of different cities and decide what had been the impact of government policy. The report drew five main lessons for future policy:

---

3. M. Parkinson, 'British Urban Strategy', in M. Parkinson and Le Gales, *National Policies for Cities in France and Britain: A Comparative Assessment* (Report to the Franco-British Council, April 1994), p. 39.

1.   The importance of creating effective coalitions of local players to attempt urban regeneration;

2.   the need to give greater opportunities to local authorities to play a significant part in such coalitions in their new roles as enablers and facilitators;

3.   the equal need for local communities to have opportunities to play a part especially because evidence of increasing polarization suggests the need for specific resources to address the scope for community capacity building;

4.   the need to improve the coherence of programmes across and within government departments, requiring strategic objectives to be identified to guide departmental priorities. Where separate programmes had been successfully linked, area targeting had played an important part.

5.   Part of such coherence must derive from better targeting of resources and this could be best done at regional level to reflect the varying constraints and opportunities across different regions and achieve more effective co-ordination across programmes and departments.

Partnership in Regeneration—City Challenge

Urban policy has undergone various changes during the 1990s. On the one hand, quantitatively, resources being directed at urban regeneration continue to shrink. On the other, the government's approach has changed partly to take into account the reduced resource base and partly to incorporate the lessons of the 1980s. Two government initiatives of the early 1990s clearly take account of these policy messages. First, City Challenge incorporated these principles. Now they are further developed in the more radical changes ushered in by the introduction of Government Offices for the Regions, the Single Regeneration Budget (SRB) and streamlined arrangements in Whitehall for promoting regeneration through a new Ministerial Committee.

City Challenge began in 1991. It was intended to be different in terms of values, organization and priorities.[4] Its aims covered not only what it was hoped would result from the programme, but also the way in which it would be delivered. The diversity of local circumstances was recognized. Priorities were to be determined, not by central government, but by local partners defining their vision for the selected area and translating

4.   See M. Parkinson, 'A New Strategy for Britain's Cities?', *Policy Studies* 14.2 (Summer 1993).

that vision into specific programmes and projects. Innovative solutions and flexible responses to old problems were encouraged. The emphasis was on tackling problems comprehensively. In contrast to the earlier focus on physical capital, City Challenge also stressed human and social capital. This holistic, area-based approach and the emphasis on decentralization marked a significant departure from the initiatives of the 1980s, which had minimized the part played by local authorities and local communities.

It is too early to judge the impact of City Challenge. The Round 1 Partnerships are only halfway through their programmes. But something can be learnt from the experience so far of the 31 City Challenges about the strengths and weaknesses of the model on the basis of the initiative's design and implementation.[5]

It has a number of distinctive characteristics. First, it is both competitive and targeted. Areas competed for the funding. This was one of the main criticisms of the initiative, plus the fact that the money was not new but top-sliced from existing programmes. When resources are short, those wanting them are always, implicitly or explicitly competing for them. What was controversial about City Challenge was not the fact of competition, but its basis. The criteria for selecting the winning bids covered both social deprivation and economic opportunity in the areas concerned. It has yet to be seen whether the results vindicate the choices made based on these projections and whether competition has resulted in the higher quality programme development and delivery intended. However, if the use of this principle is extended, it may result in an increasing divide between neighbourhoods. Those that can be aligned with strategic opportunities will be able to attract resources. Those that cannot will fail, despite—or precisely because of—their scale of need, and will fall further behind.

Government assumes that focusing a comprehensive renewal programme on a well-defined area will have a more significant impact within a five year period for the level of resources expended. This raises questions not only about whether the 'right' local authorities were selected, but also whether they had identified the most appropriate areas in their cities. Concentrating resources may be a useful counter to an authority's tendency to spread them thinly, if more even-handedly,

---

5.   The material in this section draws largely upon H. Russell, *City Challenge Interim Evaluation: Phase I Progress Report to the Steering Committee* (European Institute for Urban Affairs; Liverpool: John Moores University, June 1994).

throughout the area. But targeting can contravene local feelings about 'fairness', especially if, as is intended, additional mainstream resources are also sucked into the target neighbourhood at the cost of surrounding ones.

Targeting in City Challenge also refers to ensuring that the benefits reach the intended beneficiaries. The physical regeneration of the 1980s, while often successful in its own terms, could leave the lives of residents in adjacent areas untouched. New jobs went to outsiders; new housing was unaffordable. In City Challenge, efforts are being made to: (1) promote community economic development to make a lasting difference to the area; (2) address issues of individual development through such routes as education, training, careers advice; (3) encourage local employers to target training and job opportunities on local people; (4) improve the local quality of life economically, physically and socially; (5) involve intended beneficiaries in the policy making and implementation processes.

This last point links with another key aspect of City Challenge—partnership. Public–private partnerships have become a familiar feature of the urban regeneration landscape over recent years. City Challenge took the idea a step further: (1) recognizing that urban problems cannot be tackled singly. An effective strategy must be comprehensive and integrated; (2) returning a key role in spearheading and co-ordinating such an approach to local government; (3) appreciating that to be effective in meeting local needs and having lasting effects, any such strategy must be owned by local people. So the community is brought in as a partner.

It is worth focusing briefly on partnership more generally. Partnership can be seen in different ways—as a valuable means of bringing institutions together to address local problems and meet local challenges; or as a way of distracting attention from the resource and other constraints faced by local agencies, especially local authorities. Partnership is hard to define. There is no blueprint for partnerships' organization, terms of reference or way of working. They tend to be defined in terms of what they should be like, the quality of their aims and potential added value, rather than their structure and constitution.

Partnerships may be entered into for a variety of reasons. Partners may come together to gain funds which they could not access alone. They may assume that partnership creates synergy, that the resulting enterprise will be greater than the sum of its parts. They may see partnership as having a transformative role, changing relationships, organizational cultures and ways of thinking and working. In the case of City Challenge, government was clearly promoting partnership as a way of achieving both synergy and transformation. It held out the carrot of budget enlargement to draw people into the scheme.

For partnerships to work, they must be based on realism and trust, with a clear delineation of the roles, relationships and expectations of the partners within an organization structure appropriate to the scale and nature of the task. There should also be parity amongst the partners. This is especially difficult to achieve in relation to the community sector for a number of reasons. Defining the community is the first problem. The DoE adopts a broad view to encompass anyone who is investing his or her life in the area in any way, who has a stake and therefore wants a say in effecting change. Thus there are diverse interests and equally diverse forms of organization. And the community sector tends to merge with the voluntary sector. In practice, how City Challenge, or any project based on partnership, engages with the community must depend upon the entry points, bases of representation, that exist or can be readily created.

It is usually difficult for communities to mobilize quickly, so they were at a disadvantage when local authorities had to prepare City Challenge bids to meet very short deadlines. Some feel they are still running to catch up with the public and private sectors. Also to be overcome are problems of representivity and accountability; access to resources, including information and expertise; barriers to involvement, whether practical ones such as money, transport or childcare, or more intangible ones such as culture and confidence.

The unrelenting pace continues for Challenges as they struggle to spend their money in time and deliver their promised outputs, such as training places, jobs, houses, private sector leverage, as well as encourage maximum local participation. In the end, judgments about City Challenge must rest not only on its practical achievements but on whether it has also been able to deliver some of its wider ambitions. Has it achieved quality, innovation and local flexibility in its programmes? Has it resulted in sustainable development? Has it produced organizational arrangements which enable local authorities and communities to play more substantial strategic roles? Have other partner agencies become more responsive to local circumstances?

Although at present the government has no plans for a third round of City Challenge, many of its principles have been embodied in plans for the Single Regeneration Budget. In addition, the changes in the role and scope of local government mean that forms of partnership and collaboration are not confined to social initiatives but are relevant to the mainstream delivery of local services. Councils are having to look for new funding sources. They are having to bring new players in to provide services. New models of mixed provision are being created. At the same time, the growth of special interest groups, the increasing professionalism of local voluntary and community groups, the rising expectations of recipients of local authority services, all point towards the need for wider ownership of, and involvement in, the planning and delivery of services which vitally affect the quality of people's lives. It is important, therefore, to learn the lessons of City Challenge.

The Churches as Partners

The Bidding Guidance for the SRB says 'Bids should also aim to harness the talents and resources of the voluntary sector and volunteers and involve local communities'.[6] Clearly there are going to be increased opportunities for churches to join in regeneration initiatives. What can local churches bring to the partnership table?

1.   The churches should bring their clear value base, their understanding of both human worth and fallenness, and the moral credibility which comes from their longstanding presence in neighbourhoods under stress:

> bringing a pre-disposition to work collaboratively and recognition of what other sectors have to offer combined with realism that people have different and often conflicting interests; contributing a particular perspective to the vision of what the area might become and the steps necessary to fulfil the vision; using their direct experience of the street level impact of public policy or economic and social trends should inform the strategy; being concerned for the long term sustainability of the programme as against quick fixes.

2.   The churches' ministry should reflect the Christian gospel's concern for all people and for the whole person including the social and economic dimensions of life in their enabling and capacity building role:

---

6.   Government Offices for the Regions, *Bidding Guidance: A Guide to Funding From the Single Regeneration Budget.*

bringing awareness of both the obstacles to participation and personal development UPAs and the untapped potential; helping to build local residents' confidence and skills; making buildings and resources available to the community to support local people in their own initiatives.

3.   Churches have a role as advocates with other voluntary and community sector partners:

to underline the equity agenda which might always be in danger of being glossed over when set against commercial interests or the pressure for quick results. This entails actively pursuing equal opportunities and monitoring the redistributive effects of the programme to see if the gap is narrowing between local people and those in better off surrounding areas; to assert the need for qualitative as well as quantitative ways of evaluating the programme; to put the specific programme in context, looking more widely at the allocation of resources to areas in need.

4.   Churches may themselves provide variety of social and environmental projects, with or without outside funding, which might:

strengthen the local network of care; fill gaps in mainstream provision; allow for innovatory approaches.

Potentially, local churches have a lot to offer. However, how far this potential is fulfilled will depend upon the extent to which they are already equipped to contribute, not so much in terms of their material resources as their motivation, outlook, existing local involvement and way of working. Some questions may serve to illustrate: Does the church itself allow for full participation? Churches and their leaders are just as prone as other agencies to impose solutions on others, to think they know best, to undertake meaningless so-called consultation exercises, to act *for* instead of *with* people. Is this type of local involvement and action fully integrated with the worshipping life of the church or is it a matter of running two sorts of organizations—and possibly with different participants—alongside each other with little interchange? Are the implications of this local way of working being taken on board by the wider Church and influencing its priorities, deployment of resources, organization and mission? Two-way communication is required. Very often local churches or branches of sector ministry complain that they are overlooked or misunderstood. But they must articulate what they are doing and show its relation to the Church's wider ministry if they are to effect more deep seated change in the Church itself.

THE COAL CAMPAIGN 1992–93:
THE INTERACTION OF FAITH AND ECONOMICS

Tony Attwood

The Coal Crisis

The Coal Closure Plan

On 13 October 1992 the President of the Board of Trade, the Rt Hon. Michael Heseltine MP, announced to Parliament that 31 of British Coal's 50 deep mine collieries would close within a matter of months. This shut-down of over 60% of capacity would make 30,000 miners' jobs redundant. The privatized electricity generating companies had already made known that new contracts with British Coal would be for much reduced tonnages. The news was far worse than expected. It was devastating. The whole country was stunned.

Suddenly, the general public were supporting the miners' cause and calling for an integrated energy policy. Mr Heseltine insisted he was being very responsible because the requirement for British Coal's output was so much smaller. The news media reflected popular feeling. Nevertheless, now the country is relying increasingly on imported coal and scarce, valuable natural gas for the generation of electricity. Vast quantities of coal have been sterilized in the ground, perhaps for ever, amounting to billions of pounds worth of electricity equivalent. Nearly two years later even more collieries have been closed. So it seems that the campaign to slow down, halt or even reverse, the plan was actually a failure. This paper evaluates that endeavour from the position of the churches.

'Sheer Madness'

Of twelve collieries in South Yorkshire, nine were to cease production. (The three 'surviving' pits are now closing but four others are being operated independently with a much smaller workforce.) The Bishop of Sheffield, the Rt Revd David Lunn, with a Northumbrian background and 13 years' ministry in South Yorkshire, knew the traumas mining communities faced when pits drew their last tonne. Even in the mid-

1980s over 26,000 miners had been employed in this area. More than half of those jobs had already been lost. The Bishop was interviewed on the one o'clock news, before Mr Heseltine's statement to the House of Commons. He spoke of the 'sheer madness' of wasting precious natural assets.[1] Mr Heseltine was soon to find that he had touched a raw nerve, and the Bishop had caught the mood of the nation. On this subject the churches acted together and played a formative role in a campaign of resistance.

Change: Crisis and Opportunity

The Government's closure plan unleashed several crises. The opposition in Parliament and in the country was so great that the government was in some doubt as to whether it could defend the measure successfully. To have lost the vote on so sensitive an issue would indeed have been a disaster. By a deft political manoeuvre, the Department of Trade and Industry split the list of closures. Ten pits would be the subject of a statutory consultation; the prospects for the remaining 21 were to be reviewed. A select committee would examine evidence as well as the department itself. By this means the support of the great majority of the government's own substantial coal lobby of 30 MPs was ensured, but the vote was still tight.

The plan precipitated a crisis for mining people. The 1991 census returns now reveal that in the Toll Bar district of Bentley in Doncaster, for example, male unemployment was already 30%. By 1992 in South Yorkshire the number of 'men on books' was down to about 500 at most collieries. A wages bill of around £14m was being delivered into each community. The money going into people's bank accounts to save for house improvements and holidays, or into their pockets and out into the local economy would now be severely curtailed. The impact will bite for years to come.

The churches also faced a crisis because of their long-standing commitment to these communities. Uniquely among the UK's coalfield areas, the South Yorkshire and Selby Coalfields are twentieth-century developments. In the case of the former, local churches grew up with the newly increased populations as the pits were sunk and the coal mined.[2]

---

1.   Press Release from the Bishop of Sheffield, 13 October 92.
2.   A. Rodgers, 'The Church's Mission amid Development and Change in the Mining Industry and Communities of South Yorkshire, 1990', in 'God's Coal', compiled by T. Attwood, p. 7.

Local congregations were, naturally, interested in wider social and economic aspects. Between 1987 and 1990 six training days for local clergy and lay leaders were held to strengthen this interest. Each drew an average of 25 people from different churches, encouraging an ecumenical approach at the grass roots. The churches were also ready at area and national levels to challenge what many believed was the irresponsible loss of invaluable resources.

The Churches' Reaction and Failure

Within a week of Mr Heseltine's announcement 600 congregations in South Yorkshire contributed to a petition asking for an urgent review of the closure plan. By the time the petition was sent to Westminster it included 70,000 signatures. The chairman of the Sheffield District of the Methodist Church, the Revd Bryan Rippin, as Chairman of the South Yorkshire Ecumenical Council spoke for all the churches at a public meeting. Meanwhile the Roman Catholic Bishop of Hallam, the Rt Revd Gerald Moverley, issued an open letter to be read in the churches of his diocese, including all of South Yorkshire. Vehement indignation was shown up and down the land. There were two major rallies in London. The president of the NUM, Arthur Scargill, received favourable interviews and comments.

The government was shaken. When members of the Network of Coal Industry Chaplains, together with the Bishop of Sheffield, met the Energy Minister, Tim Eggar MP, they heard that if the furore had been anticipated the plans would have been set out in another way. The manner in which the government has achieved its objective is not a sign of failure by the opposition, including that of the churches, but rather the vindication of a principled and well-grounded stand. The reasons behind the churches' effective response offer a good example of the interaction of faith and economics.

An Effective Response:
The Work of Industrial Mission in South Yorkshire

For the Industrial Mission in South Yorkshire the coal crisis was an important time to show the combination of belief and action. As the coalfield chaplain, I was particularly involved. When Christian witness was imperative, ideas and reality became one.

Common Ground

There was common ground. Faith is about God's love in action, economics (*oikonomia* in Greek) is to do with housekeeping, the good stewardship of the resources that God has given in creation. Despite different traditions and backgrounds, the ecumenical movement has witnessed a growing unanimity of view between the main Christian traditions on matters concerning the sustainability of the *oikoumene*, the whole habitable earth.

Faith is the source, driving force and common goal of the ecumenical movement. This movement seeks visible unity in the faith of the Lord Jesus Christ as God and Saviour according to the Scriptures. Economics is concerned with the production, distribution and consumption of material goods and services. Forty years ago the Evanston Assembly of the World Council of Churches acknowledged the legitimate interest of Christian faith in these economic processes because of God's care for the human beings involved. In 1975 the advisory group on economic matters within the Commission on the Churches' Participation in Development reaffirmed the place of this interest on the ecumenical agenda by noting 'the call to resist the totalitarianism of the market through confessing the (sovereignty) of Christ'.[3] More recently the Papal Encyclical 'Centesimus Annus' has detailed the understanding that profit is not the only regulator of a business, 'other human and moral factors must also be considered'. In the long term these are 'at least equally important for the life of a business'.[4]

Christian Values

There was a new sense of the relevance of Christian values about creation, covenant and community. The interaction of theology and practice is envisaged in the Anglican Synodical Government Measure 1969. Churches and parishes are to 'promote in the Deanery the whole mission of the Church, pastoral, evangelistic, social and ecumenical'. Members are now expecting to see these connections being made through their area Synod, as well as in the life of their own local church. The threat to the few remaining mining communities presented a test case.

Adwick-le-Street deanery, to the north-west of Doncaster included three collieries in its area until Brodsworth closed in 1990 and Askern in

3. N. Lossky, *et al.*, *Dictionary of the Ecumenical Movement* (Geneva: WCC, 1991).

4. John Paul II, *'Centesimus Annus'* (1991), p. 26.

1991. In September 1992, some three weeks before Mr Heseltine's announcement, the Deanery Synod discussed the Report of the Archbishops' Commission 'Faith in the Countryside'. The coalfield chaplain also serves as rural dean and in this capacity I drew attention to the section on Mining Communities.[5] The meeting unanimously agreed a motion deploring the prospect of a hasty run-down in the coal mines of South Yorkshire and resolved to urge the Diocesan Synod and the General Synod to call for a re-think of government energy policy. People were especially anxious about Bentley, the last pit in the deanery.

Effective Organization

The churches were able to act because of effective organization. This was a new dimension for mission, but the churches, having done their theological homework, had an interest in seeing faith at work in relation to economic life. A matter affecting people's livelihood had wrongly appeared to be wholly in the secular or amoral domain. Energy policy and the future of mining communities was now recognized as a proper subject for the Church to consider and to work on in partnership with other concerned organizations.[6]

The proposed motion for the Diocesan Synod from Adwick-le-Street deanery was duly considered by the Bishop's council but was not included in the agenda because the situation was so uncertain. The immediate response took priority because the meeting occurred on the evening of the day the closure plan was announced. Urgent action was agreed in a proposal that the Churches Together in South Yorkshire be asked to circulate a petition to all member churches. A draft text was agreed and the news media were informed of the council's unanimous endorsement of the Bishop's remarks earlier that day.

5.   Archbishops' Commission on Rural Areas, 'Faith in the Countryside' (1990), p. 69.

6.   Industrial Mission in South Yorkshire was a key agency in a range of contacts which the churches undertook at every level, including the Churches Council for Britain and Ireland, County Ecumenical Bodies and church leaders, Church Action on Poverty and social responsibility officers. IMSY was generally recognized as co-ordinating the response. With the help of a Church Army student on placement, IMSY became a clearing house for information, including the despatch of a 'Pit Action Pack' published by the Sheffield District of the Methodist Church. Coal chaplains were in regular touch with all sections of the industry, management and trades unions, MPs, local authorities, the Coalfield Communities Campaign, local churches and community groups.

Integrated Mission

The specific contribution of Industrial Mission was shown by the capacity to unite Christian faith and values with effective organization in order to deliver the objective of reversing the closure plan. Although unsuccessful at the time and unable to change the prevailing ideology that the market is necessarily the best arbiter of energy needs, Industrial Mission was a key agent in enabling the churches to question this belief and draw attention to the debate about whether the market was really free. The growing scarcity of energy resources will in time provide sharp evidence of the moral and practical deficiency in government energy policy.

Encouraged by the remarkable degree of agreement in opposition to the closure plan, the coalfield chaplain received further support in the Industrial Mission staff meeting. As I filled out the news stories with more detailed information, colleagues realized that faith and economics had come together here. A positive response was required. The churches' commitment to further people's well-being meant applying more than purely short term market-led considerations to the coal industry. Theological principles and pastoral experience advocated an integrated energy policy. Plans were made about letters to MPs, lobbying by church leaders in coalfield areas and in constituencies whose MPs were members of the Conservative Coal Group. Churches in the coalfield communities of South Yorkshire would be invited to regular meetings for prayer, information exchange and mutual support. A representative group would consider our response to the government's review process. A National Conference for Coalfield Churches would decide on future ecumenical action.[7]

Meanwhile, the 300 members of the Industrial Mission Association were alerted to the expected attack on the coal industry. The October 1992 newsletter to industrial chaplains, lay members and officers in the social responsibility departments of the churches carried an inset from the National Network of Coal Industry Chaplains. Vigilance was urged because of the need for good stewardship of all the resources involved:

---

7.   This was held in Sheffield on 30 January 1993 and addressed by the Bishop of Durham, the Rt Revd David Jenkins. The chairman of the Trade and Industry Select Committee, Richard Caborn MP, presented his Committee's Report. The Conference endorsed the recommendations as the most likely way of securing the future of the largest number of pits, but Parliament was not able to debate it fully. The Department of Trade and Industry's own report, 'The Prospects for Coal', was published two months later and voted on in just four days.

the skill and experience of miners; the coal, occurring naturally and freely in the ground; and the capital investment in equipment, backed up by research and development in mining techniques and the efficient use of coal in a wide range of industrial processes.[8]

The Achievement of Ecumenical Co-operation

The government's policy of 'the market will decide', with its devastating impact for communities shattered by the loss of the industry which was their life, had coalesced with new practical forms of ecumenical thinking and involvement in mission. Across South Yorkshire, church congregations and Christian leaders joined people throughout the country to challenge the hegemony of narrow market-led economics and advocate a better stewardship of resources. We caught a glimpse of a Church which is truly ecumenical, integrating faith and the reality of people's lives. We must now consider the relevance of this response for a proper understanding of the mission of the Church.

The Mission of the Church

Limitations to Face

The coal campaign did not succeed in changing policy, but the churches had a part in a movement which resulted in a different approach via the extensive review of the closure programme. The government still won the day but this is not to say that the churches were ineffective. Two

---

8.   Regular briefings were produced for the IMA Newsletter and made available for church leaders, MPs, local and national media. The National Network of Coal Industry Chaplains made submissions to the Department for Trade and Industry and the select committees for Trade and Industry and Employment. The Council of Industrial Mission in South Yorkshire happened to be holding its Annual General Meeting on 25 March, the day the government produced 'The Prospects for Coal'. A response was sent from the meeting. At its next ordinary meeting in June 1993, a call was made for the select committee report to be debated. This took place in the House of Commons in July. There was a further debate in October—all to no avail. On this occasion, I had the privilege of sharing a platform with the Rt Hon. John Smith, then leader of the opposition, and addressing a meeting in the Grand Committee Room. The Chaplains' Network also developed these concerns with German colleagues working with the churches in the Ruhr Valley. A set of resolutions about coal and energy policy in the European Union were agreed in May 1993. They were used as the basis for a series of meetings later that autumn in Brussels with officers of the European Commission concerning the future of the industry, mining communities and the role of the Church.

main lessons were learnt about what is possible.

First, there is an enormous difficulty about changing the mind of a determined government. The view that the government had long been set on excising the National Union of Mineworkers from any effective role in industrial relations or political life now has much greater support. The 'dirty' image of coal and the cost of making the coal for electricity generation cleaner have been added to loaded economic arguments to fulfil this overriding political aim. Thus at electricity privatization in 1988, nuclear generation was set at 18% of demand, protected by a subsidy levied on electricity bills while coal has been the main fuel. New gas generation plant has been sanctioned well ahead of demand, secured by 15 year take or pay contracts. Britain's leading role in coal research and technology and the opportunity to develop high-efficiency combined heat and power systems have all been sacrificed. Meanwhile, we now know that there are, after all, industrial and domestic markets which British Coal had not been able, or was not allowed, to supply. The cost of the closure programme to people, communities and long-term energy availability is incalculable.

Secondly, there is the need for unity about an issue in order to organize a strong campaign. That the Industrial Mission in South Yorkshire and elsewhere, together with agencies for social responsibility within the churches were able to co-ordinate support was only possible, as Paul Bagshaw has pointed out, 'because Church leaders and Church congregations shared the political will to campaign'.[9]

Achievements to Build on
First, the coal crisis showed the Church at its best because the importance of having a Christian presence in every community and at significant points in our social and economic life was widely recognized. Christian activism about people's livelihoods and the future of communities thrived in an atmosphere made tense by the succession of dramatic announcements about redundancies, reviews and reprieves. People had not been asked about the upheaval wrought by the introduction of coal-mining. Once again, life-changing decisions were being made over the heads of those most concerned. There were united prayer vigils and marches with church banners. No speaker's platform was complete without a representative of the churches. News items often carried a comment

9.   P. Bagshaw, *The Church beyond the Church* (Sheffield: IMSY, 1994), p. 124.

from a church leader. The incarnation of God's love had a new meaning.

Secondly, the heightened awareness of a political context for ministry provided a situation in which the dynamics of Church life were seen to operate effectively. Christian presence in the communities, at the pit gates, talking with coal industry officials in management and the trades unions, speaking in the media and at meetings, lobbying the politicians, had a sharp, practical, human edge. This was no short-term expedient crusade. It was spirituality at work. The unity of belief and practice was founded on theological rigour and pastoral compassion. The churches were witnessing to the interaction of faith and economics to secure for people God's justice and peace. The integrity of creation was being sought in a challenge to market economics by the call for a stewardship of resources which took seriously long-term energy needs, environmental considerations and people in economically depressed circumstances. A change in the accepted order was needed. The redemption of the world by Jesus Christ opened up another way. We were engaged in God's mission.

Questions for Urgent Attention
This evaluation of the Church's notable contribution to the coal campaign and the lessons for the Church's mission which can be drawn from it raise some leading issues about the recognition of expertise and the deployment of resources in ministry:

1. The Church's endeavours were not only limited by government intentions, they were dependent on a knowledge of the social and economic situation surrounding the coal industry and mining communities.
2. A crucial element in the Church's witness was an ability to galvanize the prayers and the genuine concerns into action that had the passion and vitality of an effective response.
3. The Industrial Mission was the source of many of the details of this knowledge and ability, offering a unique capacity to unite and activate the various factors in the situation.
4. The ingredients for mission which the Industrial Mission provides include a ministry at the place of employment; analyses of the powers at work and the human effects of events; engagement with all people concerned; and the encouragement of church leaders and congregations to express the Christian interest in worship and action. In the coal crisis all these ingredients have shown their true worth for the Church's mission.

For the Church to advance its mission about energy policy and the future of mining communities, a like commitment to that shown throughout the coal campaign is required. It is a vital role for a changing society, 'to base our community life and our values, and to nurture the soul of our civilisation, on more enduring realities'.[10] Industrial Mission is putting energy into this crucial witness. The work is ecumenical and contextual; the ministry, pastoral and prophetic.

10. The Archbishop of York, the Most Revd and Rt Hon. John S. Habgood in a sermon on 6 May 1990 during an exhibition in the Parish Church of St George, Doncaster, marking the work of the churches in the South Yorkshire coalfield.

SPEAKING AS WE FIND:
WOMEN'S EXPERIENCE OF TYNESIDE INDUSTRY

Caroline Barker Bennett

Industrial Mission has never majored on women. Its beginnings were bound up with the Church's need to make contact with working class men, the group most absent from congregations. Industrial Mission has tended to have an ambivalent attitude to power. On the one hand, it has sought to influence decision makers and making in discreet ways; on the other, it has shunned clerical authority and desired to be in solidarity with shop floor workers. Shop floor workers who reflect on their situation and who are willing to take on leadership roles in trades unions have been natural allies of Industrial Mission.

Women workers are on the whole very powerless. Their responsibilities at home make it difficult for them to play leading roles in trades unions. They tend, certainly in the north east, to work in industries with predominantly female workforces, in clothing and food for example, where the trades unions have been weak. So women workers have not fallen into categories which industrial chaplains have particularly cultivated—managers with influence and responsibility; active trades unionists. Add to this the fact that most industrial chaplains have been male clergy, and it is not surprising that women workers' concerns and gifts were neglected. Then, from the late seventies, a number of women industrial chaplains came on the scene and the women's movement woke people up to issues that had been below the surface.

When I went to Tyneside in 1977, part of the job was to visit an engineering works, 'James's', which had a considerable number of women in its workforce. These women were in an unusual situation since they worked alongside men in a highly unionized workplace and therefore participated in a union structure which had power. The women shop stewards who went on courses and met other women stewards were always amazed to find how much better off they were than those in largely female workforces.

These advantages only became clear to me slowly. When I first went there I was much more aware of how unpleasant the jobs were and how drab the surroundings. The only bright spots were the great water boilers strategically placed for people to make tea! I was astonished at how many individual operations the making of oil seals entailed and how much was done by hand. The factory makes seals from metals and rubber mixes and the manufacturing process includes moulding, trimming and inspecting. Inspection was the highest grade of job done by women. It required keen eyesight and continued concentration to spot tiny flaws in multifarious seals for uses including car and aircraft engines. Other jobs done by women included operating punching and knifing machines and pulling flash off moulded parts. None of these jobs was intrinsically interesting and some were physically unpleasant. At least you could often talk to others as you worked.

I was struck by the fact that those who did cramping jobs did not become cramped as people. Often they had gifts and skills which, given other circumstances, might have led them to better paid, more esteemed jobs. This was particularly true for the women for whom the route via apprenticeships to 'skilled' work and possibly management, had not been open.

Alongside this experience of visiting an engineering works I also started visiting 'Marie Sutherland', a women workers' co-operative manufacturing clothes. Here were women who had worked as machinists in clothing factories and who had no management experience beyond that gained from running a home and family (usually underrated skills), who were attempting to enter a notoriously volatile market, albeit one ever-present as an employer of women in the north east.

Reflecting on these experiences led me to undertake a research project to explore how some of the women I knew had come to their present job; what they had done when they left school and how their lives as workers had developed. I decided not to include details about their home lives unless these were mentioned by them and clearly relevant. This was partly in order to keep the focus on their experience as workers and partly because I thought they might feel happier about having a conversation recorded which would not explore private and possibly sensitive matters. I recorded conversations with nineteen women who had left school and started work between 1934 and 1981. Because the openings for women on Tyneside were relatively few, what emerged out of their accounts was a history of women's employment on Tyneside during the period.

So what were some of the main findings of the project? Clearly it is not possible to encompass here all that came out of the study particularly since a major element of it was to record what the women said in conversation about their experience and this was naturally discursive. In order to give a flavour of the method and the findings, I offer here a few headlines and quotations.

Careers Advice and Starting Work

For thirty years after the war jobs were easy to come by, while at the beginning and end of the period they were not. However, in other ways things changed remarkably little. The range of jobs available to working class girls leaving school at the minimum age was remarkably consistent: shop, factory and office work and hairdressing were constants with, in the thirties, domestic service.

Margaret, leaving school in 1939, reported,

> We did have people come to ask what we would like to be when we were leaving... They'd ask you, 'Would you like to be typing or hairdressing or such as a domestic?' Although they asked me if I'd be a domestic and I definitely said 'No! Emphatically, No!' But I've ended up that way!

(She had taken a job as a hospital cleaner after thirty years as a supervisor in James's ended in redundancy).

Pat, leaving school in 1981, said,

> Oh aye, we got careers advice. But what I wanted they didn't take lessons in it. So I never bothered taking any exams and I started in my factory (clothing) on the YOP two days after leaving school... I wanted painting and decorating but they didn't have it.

Brenda, who eventually became assistant convenor at James's, left school in 1957. Her mother was a decisive influence in preventing her from starting on a career which might have led to promotion.

> I fancied being a prison wardress when I left school and I wrote away for the information. But it was Mam who wouldn't let us go. She said, 'Some queer characters get in there and you're not going to be punched around and badly used'. So needless to say, it all went into the fire.

Instead a relative spoke for her and she started in the Co-op greengrocery.

Shop work was favoured by several mothers on the grounds that it was clean and respectable without the stigma of factory work. In practice those who worked in shops and then moved to factory work, often when they were getting married and needed more money, felt that conditions in shops were worse than in factories. In shops, with no union to support you, you could be exploited by the manager and wages were poor. Brenda, reflecting on her experience said,

> I'll be honest with you, the time I had in the two shops—give me factory people any time. They're down-to-earth, they're not selfish, they're very kind. And I just think they're a different type of people. And I don't know how people can get the idea that factory lasses are coarse and horrible and vulgar and rude. All right, you might get the odd one or two bad people... But I still prefer yet factory people to shop people.

One of the most vivid recollections of her first job was Vera's. She went, in 1935, to join her mother who worked in 'the smoke house', or kippering shed, on the fish quay in North Shields. She described the privations of working in very cold conditions on work which was always casual and dependent on the catch and the tide.

> There was an awful lot of hardship to the point where women were pregnant, married women. Now I've worked in a yard where a woman was working. She's taken her labour, the boss has had to put her in the lorry, take her home. Within a few hours that woman has had her baby. Within a few hours, we'll say a day, that woman has been back working because times were such in those days—no work, no money. The baby was brought to work with her in the pram and it used to be a communal pram... If you had a good boss he would let the pram stand in the office to keep the baby reasonably warm. And the mother, when it needed feeding, she used to have to go and wash her hands, remove her oil skins, sit and feed her baby and there it went on.

She looked back on her time on the quay with affection because of the comradeship but, having worked in a torpedo factory during the war, she opted afterwards for the easier life of the factory where 'you had your hands washed and you sat down and you had your cup of tea and your cigarette'.

Factory Life
While working to earn is obviously of primary importance to all workers, whether men or women, the attractions of factory work for women have not been much explored. To work in a factory brings membership of a community, and this can be particularly important for

women who otherwise may have little opportunity to belong to groups outside the home. The women I talked with found it difficult to justify doing things which met their own needs. They were always worried about how their children, husbands, parents might be affected by what they did, even when it was taking a job. Working in a factory gave them access to a ready-made community which could meet a complex of needs. In a factory you have to spend time with other adults, unencumbered by children; you can ask advice and get information; there is access to cheap goods and services; you can place a bet without going to a betting shop—which some women would be loathe to do; you can consult the nurse about a health problem without bothering the doctor. In terms of contribution, it is women who are responsible for most factory celebrations. They provide the food and organize decorations. They send cards and keep in touch with those on the sick.

The Use of Women's Skills Management

It is not surprising that women reproduce at work the roles they play in the family, but what about their skills and any management gifts they may have? Here the evidence from my research was depressing. In the period after the war there were large sections of women workers at James's and therefore women supervisors. As the workforce shrunk in the eighties and departments were amalgamated, these women were squeezed out. Several of the older women I talked with had had experience as supervisors, at James's or other factories. They all preferred the role when it enabled them to join in with the work as a 'working supervisor'. Phyllis who went as a supervisor in a sweet factory said,

> I felt surplus... After coming from Faber's and having a full day and always busy, I took very badly with just standing around watching... But after a while—I got so that, well, I would mix sweets up if they were doing jars and what-not, and I got so that I filled the time in great.

Margaret started as a 'working supervisor' at James's but with the advent of a stricter piecework scheme her role became that of arbitrator of work and wages.

> I found when this piecework came in people were eating it, drinking it and sleeping it, and I found it was getting to me. Because I was saying to myself, 'Now that person got treble time yesterday; that person didn't. I'll have to work it so it balances itself out'... They say that once you come

out of work you should sever yourself, forget about it. But it's hard to put it out of your mind, you know, if you find you've slipped up and someone's been on a cushy job all day.

The women's views on management were in favour of those who had come up from the shop floor and therefore knew the work from the inside but who did not give themselves airs. Harry Joy was a legendary factory manager at James's,

> He used to come down and talk to you as if you had lived next door to him for years... If you were outside having a social event, he didn't segregate himself. He walked around. He was a good manager, Harry Joy. I'm saying he was a good manager. He might not have been a good manager as to production, but he was more for the workers. I mean, he started when he was 14, served his time. He grew up practically with the men.

Shop Stewards

Being a shop steward was the other role in which the women I talked with had an outlet for their management skills. For Brenda, as assistant convenor, the role was her main preoccupation both at work and at home. The person who gave the most vivid description of what the role entailed was Jeanette. She valued the pastoral opportunities it brought and went on,

> But they think you know everything about law; you're a mathematician. And you acquire these overnight, Caroline. It's not that you've been to any school. One day you're normal and the next day you're a mathematician, definitely; you're a marriage guidance counsellor; you're a policeman because you know all about fines and everything, going to court. Overnight you know everything! And if you don't know, I mean, they're very disappointed!

She identified being a scapegoat, 'They like someone to blame' as being a key part of the role. Her analysis raises interesting questions about the relationship of the role to that of priesthood. When I asked what had given her the ability to carry out this demanding role she replied, as a single parent, 'I think it was because I had *really* to look after Elizabeth'—not a response a male shop steward would be likely to make!

Working in a Co-operative

It might seem that to work in a women's co-operative would be a solution to the lack of opportunity offered to women in capitalist industry. In some ways it was. It was moving to see women who had no training and little experience in management gaining confidence in interviewing bank managers and negotiating deals. Needless to say surviving in the rag trade was tough and the history of Marie Sutherland has been turbulent. Contrasting views came from the members:

> When I first started I was just dismayed. I just couldn't make head nor tail of the place. There was June and Alice and they were the bosses and Paul Cane was there and he was the boss and I used to think, 'My God, I've never worked in a place like this before in my life', I mean, you had the boss and the workers—not everybody was the boss! (Julie)

> For all the ups and downs it's better working for yourselves than working for someone else. (June).

> I mean, it's not right. They should have a boss in here, definitely. (Pam).

June, looking back said,

> I think it's because of the way we fought for it. I don't know if it goes for all of them but I know I can speak for Beryl, Alice and myself (the original members still involved at the time)—we've got a commitment to the co-op you know, and there's a lot of people that helped w' and we don't want to let them down. I mean there's many a time we could have said 'to pot with it' you know, but we wouldn't, I wouldn't.

Realism and determination were the positive qualities which Marie Sutherland brought out in the members. Inter-personal conflicts and conflicts about policy were the most damaging to its life and success. In this, of course, it was no different from any other organization. Capitalist industry in western democracy evolved the highly ritualized structure of management/trades union power to cope with the sharp disputes which Marie Sutherland had to handle raw.

A THEOLOGICAL CRITIQUE OF ORCHARD PARK
AND NORTH HULL ENTERPRISES

Chris Percy

This paper brings together theology and the secular world in an attempt to discern God's activity in the local economy. The context is industrial mission in Hull. The project studied, Orchard Park and North Hull Enterprises (OPNHE), is a company limited by guarantee which was set up jointly by Hull City Council, Humberside County Council, the private sector of industry and the local community. The aim was to provide a centre of economic activity in an area of high unemployment.

The story of OPNHE is one subject of the paper; the other is a tradition of social theology which has developed in North America and Britain over the last sixty years. Contributors whose work is considered here are Reinhold Niebuhr, Ronald Preston, Philip Wogaman, David Jenkins and John Atherton. The theology provides clues for understanding the story of OPNHE as part of God's project.

The Story of OPNHE

OPNHE was set up in 1989 and during 1990 a member of North Humberside Industrial Mission (NHIM) was invited to join its advisory group. In 1990 the Mission had been relaunched with the declared aim of working not only with established firms and institutions, but in relation to innovators and the voiceless. The involvement with OPNHE enabled us to follow a story of economic regeneration by the City Council with and on behalf of voiceless people. Unemployment rates were rising at the time. By 1992 the average for Britain as a whole was 11%, for the Hull travel to work area 12% and for Hull city 16%. This affected people particularly in the city centre and on the outer estates such as Orchard Park and North Hull, where the rates were even higher.

In January 1993, at a meeting of the Hull Unemployment Trust, Bob

Edmondson the new general manager of OPNHE reviewed its progress and prospects. OPNHE's design and constitution were the work of a joint City and County Economic Initiative working party, which had included representatives of the private and the voluntary sectors. Financial and other support for the project were provided by the Urban Programme, the city and county councils, Business in the Community, the Department of Employment and private sector companies including United Biscuits, Northern Foods, Fenner and BP.

Membership of its board reflected the composition of this partnership. In November 1992 it included four local residents elected at the annual general meeting. It was to be a partnership with the community, was designed to produce real economic improvements there and to have a clear local identity. The advisory group enabled OPNHE to consult with other agencies. At that time the company employed a manager and 29 staff, three of whom were Urban Programme funded and all of whom came from the estate. A job placement manager had been seconded to OPNHE by the Employment Service. OPNHE was running a local job centre, supporting new businesses, advising people about employment and enterprise issues, managing work spaces, setting up community business and offering space to other groups for training events. Bob Edmondson considered that two innovatory features of OPNHE made it an important pilot project nationally as well as locally. One was the partnership which set it up and runs it. Private sector support for a local authority initiative of this sort had rarely been achieved. The second important feature was OPNHE's focus on the needs of local people, which had been researched by a firm of consultants. This revealed that two thirds of the unemployed people on the estate had no formal qualifications, skill or trade. People who had been interviewed said that they would like the opportunity to improve the environment of their estate. Since then the project has been provided with a new two storey building containing offices and extra work spaces. (OPNHE had started in a county council building on a former school site; work spaces had been added later.) Capital expenditure has totalled over £1 million. The plan is that OPNHE should gradually become self supporting by renting work space and developing community business. The next developments are likely to be a social club and a credit union. Meanwhile the Citizens' Advice Bureau and Disability Rights Advice Service have been established within OPNHE and there is also a cafe.

The roots of the project go back to 1985 when the working party was established. During that long gestation, issues of power and control, the importance and feasibility of community business, the social and economic priorities were thoroughly discussed. There was an important disagreement about whether community business or managed workspaces for new small businesses should be started first. Only a minority of those questioned in the skills survey were interested in starting their own business. But it was decided to build workspaces first and progress to community business later. An economic priority was to establish business that connected with the wider market, rather than confining activity to the market provided by the immediate community. OPNHE later recruited people to work for the Housing Action Trust in North Hull, which was in effect to start a community business. However this came to an end when the HAT decided to recruit its own workers. Another important decision was to constitute the board of OPNHE so that it was independent of any and all of its supporters, including the city council.

A Protestant Tradition of Social Theology

Reinhold Niebuhr gave shape and direction to this tradition as well as its original impetus, when in the 1930s his ethical concern for the car workers and unemployed people in Detroit drove him to explore the theologial basis for Christian social ethics. He found this in the doctrines of the person and work of Christ and of the nature and destiny of humankind. In the course of his exploring he engaged with romantic and rationalist philosophies of history, including Marxism, and in criticizing them showed how the kingdom of God is relevant to every historical period. He related the doctrines of creation, resurrection, second coming and judgment to the historical process of conflict in the struggle for justice and peace.

Niebuhr's experience as a pastor in Detroit made him aware of the 'irrelevance of the mild moralistic idealism, which (he) had identified with the Christian faith, to the power realities of our modern technical society'.[1] The dilemma he faced was the difficulty of working for social justice when the victims of injustice were not in the congregation, but those who benefited most from the system paid his wages. The theoretical problem he faced was the failure of liberal protestantism to offer exploited workers any alternative to Marxism. An individualistic pre-

---

1. *Reinhold Niebuhr, 1892–1971* (ed. E.J. Tinsley; London: Epworth, 1973), p. 35.

sentation of Christian faith could not respond to the social conditions of the 1930s. A political morality was needed that combined the insights of political realism—the necessity of coercion—with the insights of moral idealism. Conflict was inevitable; futile conflict must be avoided if possible.

Niebuhr wrote of the ethics of Jesus that their framework of myth functioned in a way that maintained the hope of social fulfilment while indicating that its achievement is impossible through human resources.[2] The parameters of his own system of coherence are God the creator of existence and God the fulfiller of existence; this was his non-rational framework for ethics.

According to Gordon Harland the central concern of Niebuhr's work was to relate 'Christian faith and social responsibility, *agape* and the struggle for social justice'.[3] His thinking is christocentric; the ethical norm is discerned in Christ's cross. The relation between *agape* and mutual love is shown to be dialectical, completing the incompleteness of mutual love and contradicting our achievements of love in so far as they are sinful. Humanity can only understand itself from a point beyond itself. True self understanding starts from the faith that we are known and loved by God and must find ourselves in terms of obedience to the divine will. The *agape* of the cross is no alien norm imposed from outside but the very law of our nature.

Justice is not defined by Niebuhr; it is a relational term. Love and justice are never simply the same thing; but if they must be distinguished, they can yet never finally be separated. Love demands justice; love also negates justice. Love is the source of the norm justice; and also the perspective from which its limitations can be seen. Love fulfils justice. Only love can reveal and meet the special need.

The insights which delineate justice are derived from reason, and the task of securing it is a never ending political struggle. This struggle can never be dissociated from efforts to secure a more equal distributing of power in society. The need for liberty is real but must be held in tension with the need for equality.

The meaning of history is discerned by faith. The kingdom of God is always relevant to human societies. Niebuhr wrote: 'It hovers over

---

2. R. Niebuhr, *Reflections on the End of an Era* (New York: Charles Scribner's Sons, 1934).

3. G. Harland, *The Thought of Reinhold Niebuhr* (Oxford: Oxford University Press, 1960), p. x

every moment of history in judgement and in revelation of the indeterminate possibilities of history'.[4]

Ronald Preston has taken up the issue of working for social justice by consistently advocating the formulation and use of middle axioms as a tool in Christian social ethics. These can connect the general statement of the ethical demands of the gospel with decisions that have to be made in concrete situations. They thus give relevance and point to the Christian ethic. They are attempts to define the direction in which, in a particular state of society, Christian faith must express itself. Such a consensus needs to be built by bringing together people who have relevant knowledge and experience of the issue concerned. They take principles such as that *agape* demands the search for justice and relate them to what is going on in society.

Preston has always taught that there is no moving directly from the Bible to decisions in the modern world. The advantage of starting from derivative principles such as justice and equality is that non-Christians can identify with them. It is then essential to study what is going on.

Both Preston and Philip Wogaman have written about the choice of economic systems which Christians with others have to make. Wogaman suggests criteria for assessing any economic system: whether it takes material wellbeing seriously, whether it is committed to the unity of the human family, whether it values each person and is committed to individual freedom, whether it considers persons equal in a sense more basic than any inequalities that occur, and whether it takes sin seriously. Answering such questions entails a similar process to constructing middle axioms.

Preston suggested four 'considerations' for Christians thinking about economic systems. The gospel furnishes no blueprint for society, but suggests that the equality of persons in the sight of God needs to find expression in the structures of society. There is then a preferential option for the poor. The reality of sin means that people must be able to participate in decisions that affect them. And the state should have a positive role in making the good life possible.

David Jenkins has taken up Niebuhr's critique of individualistic Christianity. He quotes Niebuhr: 'the insights of Christian religion have become the almost exclusive possession of the comfortable and privileged classes'.[5] He sets himself to listen to the Marxist critique of

---

4.   Niebuhr, *Reflections*, p. 127.
5.   D.E. Jenkins, *The Contradiction of Christianity* (London: SCM Press, 1976).

Christianity: 'Marxism convicts me of sin'.[6] But while Marxism embodies important insights into exploitation and conflict, its claim to absoluteness of diagnosis and hope is rejected. Its errors are to confine humanity to history—whereas Christian faith hopes for resurrection—and to overlook the complexities of sin. It does converge at important points with the biblical and prophetic criticism of unjust treatment of the poor. And this is similar to Preston's judgment of Marxism.

Jenkins is clear about the need for Christians to engage in radical politics as well as radical spirituality. 'The basic concern of radical politics is how to enable people to be aware that they count, not how to solve their problems for them'.[7] Marginal people do not require to be helped so much as treated as partners in a common enterprise.

Jenkins writes of the doctrine of the Holy Trinity that it 'is nothing less than the confident discovery that the possibilities of men and women are the possibilities of God'.[8] Christians are thus set free to believe that love will achieve its fulfilment. As for Niebuhr, so for Jenkins, the promise of the gospel is a social vision, a community of communion.

John Atherton has recently reviewed the tradition and tried to extend it to respond to the collapse of the communist societies. He uses the idea of the common good, perhaps hearing in it an echo of Niebuhr's affirmation of common grace, the work of God outside the Church. The possibility for people to contribute to the common good depends upon a positive interpretation of rights and freedom. He agrees with Wogaman that the priority of God's grace means that rights are a precondition of participation, not a reward for it. Recognition by people of their responsibility to contribute is equally important; human beings develop through a mutual giving and receiving.

He reviews the tradition of Christian thought about economic systems. Conservatives such as Brian Griffiths, radicals such as Duchrow and liberals such as Wogaman all make contributions which he wants to preserve rather than choose between. He wants to assert the independent value of the market as a God given reality, not simply a mechanism. Each of the three responses to a market economy has to be allowed to interact with the reality of poverty, environmental problems and the demand for participation in decision making. Both market and the challenges to the market are essential to the development of social justice.

6. Jenkins, *The Contradiction*, p. 34.
7. Jenkins, *The Contradiction*, p. 113.
8. Jenkins, *The Contradiction*, p. 143.

The OPNHE Story in the Light of this Tradition of Social Theology

The main themes of this theology are justice, equality, conflict, participation, community and hope. These provide ways of interpreting the story of OPNHE.

Justice as Equality

Atherton has argued that the reality of the market must be brought into creative relationship with the reality of poverty in a search for social justice. The market has to be constrained, as Preston says. Market forces on their own will not produce full employment. Hull City Council have such a strategy; they made an option for the poor. Even if it was not used in the debates, that phrase was in the mind of the leader of the Council, Patrick Doyle, who is a Roman Catholic and has read liberation theology.

The formation of new partnerships between the city council and the people of Orchard Park and North Hull, and between the local authorities and the private sector of industry also blazed a trail where power sharing is increasingly important: economic initiatives which look for government support. In the process people who have hitherto had little say in their economic future have been treated as partners in a common enterprise, and agents in their own recovery.

As Niebuhr emphasised, justice is a continuous struggle. The history of the working party revealed how some of those involved had wished to keep power in the hands of elected councillors rather than trust local people. But the constitution of OPNHE is a structure for social justice of the sort that Preston advocates.

Justice demands that similar institutions to OPNHE should exist on other estates in Hull. The finance is not now available for this, but Council policy aims to create similar partnerships where unemployment and poverty are worst.

Participation and Community

Wogaman says that the community should always listen to its poorest members because they will make it clear what is wrong with society. OPNHE represents a sustained attempt to listen to unemployed people in North Hull. As Atherton has argued, the opportunity to contribute to the common good of society by doing a job is a basic right. People have been enabled to work on their own environment through employment on the HAT scheme, to start small businesses either on the OPNHE premises or elsewhere, and to find jobs outside the immediate area through a local and friendly job centre and job club.

People have joined OPNHE and become board members, thus contributing to the running of their own company. They have enjoyed the surprising experience of being listened to by managers from private industry. The inevitable conflicts have been talked through until a consensus is reached. The possibility of consensus is one of Preston's themes. Thus OPNHE in its attractive new building creates community by enabling participation in new forms of economic life.

Hope

All the major Christian doctrines are hopeful, as Preston says, because they speak of the redemption of the world by Christ, the planting of the seed of the kingdom of God in history and the promise of fulfilment in the resurrection of all to a future in God. OPNHE is a sign of hope in Hull because it was a vision realized after much work by a new partnership, because it has had results of the kind planned for and because it has promise for the future which builds on these early results. It provides a model for co-operation in other parts of the city.

Conclusion

This theological tradition traces God's work in the world in the struggle for justice and in the creation of hope. All the theologians' studies also emphasize the building of community and the sharing of power. The creation and development of OPNHE show these themes being embodied in a continuing project. And this is good reason why Industrial Mission should try to support it.

SPIRITUALITY IN A SECULAR SOCIETY

Vernon Brooke

Spirituality

The word 'spirituality' tends to be used with at least two different meanings. It is used to indicate the general background of values, assumptions and relationships against which people live their lives. That is very close to theology. It is also used to refer to disciplines and habits which reinforce and develop the dynamics for a healthy inner climate in our lives. That is about our inner development. Both of these meanings are important and they are linked. In this paper, however, 'spirituality' will be used primarily in the second sense, but without losing touch with the first.

'Spirituality', as compared with some popular views of prayer, emphasizes our need to listen to God and to the world around, to learn and grow within ourselves, rather than just to talk to God. Spirituality can share with popular views of prayer, a tendency to become purely private, a retreat from the onslaught of a world that often seems antagonistic to spiritual development. That can include the trend to see spirituality purely in terms of personal fulfilment: important though personal fulfilment is, it can become an equivalent to the secular concern to measure everything by the media standard of fun. The privatization of spirituality isolates it from the inner dynamics of communities and society around us. It can easily reflect a theology that unwittingly confines God to church activities or to our inner lives. Spirituality should be a way of deepening our inner resources to face the world around us better.

That world, with the materialism that arises from science, technology and consumer economics, creates a tendency towards alienation between people and their inner selves, and between people and their neighbours as spiritual beings. Science and technology have much to offer that is good. At the same time, they can foster false assumptions by being used as dangerous masters rather than as valuable servants. Similarly, market economics are only one approach to regulating and measuring society's resources: it is not the only possible way, nor would everyone agree that it is the best way in every area of life (eg. health services). Science, technology and economics need an ethical and spiritual framework to ensure that they serve the real needs of humanity and the planet.

On the other hand, church activities can easily become a way to escape from the realities, pressures and alienation people experience in their lives, rather than a way to face up to the dynamics of life, both within ourselves and in the world around us. Much of the real spiritual agenda is set by the nature of life in the world. Theological and spiritual truth should be consistent with the world as secular disciplines discover it to be. Different disciplines are looking at the same world which is God's and which reflects God's nature. Spirituality needs to help tease out the values, attitudes and assumptions which lie, frequently unseen, within these secular disciplines and experiences.

The Christian view of God is of a creator who is at work within all people and all things, private and public, and whose purposes are pressed forward in these contexts. People and nature are given considerable freedom as to whether to respond to the pressure of God's creative power and love, and how to respond. That emphasizes the need for spirituality to include a place for looking for and listening to signs of God's work in us and around us. It suggests that spirituality involves a line which runs from deep inside ourselves, as the intimate place where we meet God, to the inside of people, organizations and events around us, as places where God is equally at work. It calls us to discover ways toward harmony with God and other people, and with the world of nature—harmony which will overcome the sense of alienation which we so often feel, and our own selfishness and fears. Paradoxically, the way to harmony, which is an aim rather than fully achievable, brings conflict both within ourselves and in the community, as blocks and hindrances to harmony and love have to be faced and transformed. Those who work for peace, justice and the integrity of creation are well aware of the paradox in this process.

Personal Experience

The beginnings of my own disciplines in spirituality lie in my late teens and early twenties. I was a member of a church with a hard line tradition in theology, and with habits of long and wordy prayers. As I went out to work, I began to ask questions about the system of traditional beliefs put before us which seemed inconsistent with the world as I experienced it. I was met with an apparent desire to avoid the questions. Increasingly, I felt my needs to be at odds with the church tradition—or to be more accurate, I felt there must be something wrong with me, to be different from such dedicated Christians. The exploring of my questionings and doubts is a different, though related, story. Part of that process was that I increasingly felt the saying of prayers to be telling God what God already knew better than us, while I was also finding that the 'personal' image made God too much like another human, however grand: it limited God too much to be God, in my view, and allowed no room for a sense of mystery. That, I can see now, has as much to do with my personality as with the nature of God.

At college, I began to feel that routine daily services like matins and evensong were not very helpful for me, even with college attempts to create new alternatives. That is not a criticism of those who do find daily offices a helpful way of spirituality. It was a way that was too formal and which felt too superficial for me.

For a period of several years I gave up my attempts at private prayer while finding the Eucharist increasingly important. That period was punctuated erratically by a few momentary experiences of God's over-whelming presence. They happened at a concert, on high bare hillsides, by a rough sea, and later before the power of a large steel making vessel. They were brief but disturbing experiences in which I met a sense of infinite power and was made acutely aware of my own limitations and weaknesses. It was an important part of changing a worn out and irrelevant picture of an 'Old Man upstairs' into an image of God as a creative force within all things. It also prevented the question of spirituality becoming entirely lost from view.

Subsequently, a number of influences (several of them connected with Industrial Mission work) began a process of developing new spirituality disciplines. As Industrial Mission took a fresh look at its theology in the 1970s, some of us began to feel the need for some kind of support in spirituality. I began to use impressions gleaned from management disci-plines to review the events of each day, and I read something from the Bible, sometimes a complete book. Our Industrial Mission team also began meeting over a cheese and wine supper to discuss recent events in our work in relation to a Bible passage. I established an occasional habit of looking at particular issues which arose in factory visiting, from the perspective of a God who creates order from chaos, good from evil. I also began to take regular exercise, on the assumption that if God works through material things we should try to look after our bodies.

Working from that experimental base, I developed those ideas that seemed to work and dropped those that did not. I took ideas from any source that seemed constructive. At a retreat, a bishop offered some insights from *On Consideration* by Bernard of Clairvaux.[1] In these books Bernard offered a discipline to one of his monks who became pope, to help him avoid the worst excesses of papal power. The advice is still relevant to many worldly and management situations today. It calls us to look at the influence of our own family backgrounds; to look at our organization to see how we have been using people; to look beneath the formalities and organization to see what really has been happening and how people have been using us; and then to consider the place of God within all this. Bernard then advises us to look again at ourselves. I found that circular process unavoidable. Later I replaced his considerable detail with my own summary and included some Ignatian influences.

By these kinds of means, I have gradually developed a system of meditation which I use regularly, while not legalistically, and I have other supplementary methods which I use less often. My meditation begins with silence in which I remember God's presence in all things and all people, God who gives me all I have and all I am. Then I review the previous day to look with gratitude at good things that happened; to explore dreams and fantasies, feelings and moods, uncertainties or failures, and to ask what the challenges of God might be in those things. I look both at the world around me and into myself. Next I look at the day ahead, at its potential and problems. I read through a book of the Bible over a period, noting what speaks to me and what does not, trying to see what I can understand or disagree with. I have a list of people, organizations and issues that I am particularly concerned about at any time, to seek the call of Love in relation to them. I have a time of meditation about any image or expression of God's nature and work that seems to arise from those steps. Finally I check whether there are any practical things I should do as a result.

I use a journal, a diary, to clarify my thoughts and develop these questions: it forces me to think and not just 'go through the motions'. I do not necessarily have something to say under every part of this medi-

---

1.   Bernard of Clairvaux, *On Consideration* (trans. G. Lewis; Oxford: Clarendon Press, 1908).

tation every time, but I consider each item. It is part of a wider range of habits which include occasionally finding a longer time for quiet reflection; time every few weeks reviewing my work, relationships and feelings with a spiritual companion; and physical exercise. The process of development still continues.

Contexts and Differences

When reading about the links between personality types and the different methods of spirituality, I was surprised at how many of the suggestions it made for my personality were things I had discovered by experiment. Two lessons seem to flow from that. First, it is worth experimenting to find out what works for us. I have also noted that some disciplines which we do not naturally accept can be helpful. I have, in recent years, begun to explore my sensual side, a strange experience for an intuitional thinker. Secondly, we should note that there is no single correct way in spiritual disciplines: different people need different approaches.

A group of non-stipendiary ministers revealed methods that included weight-lifting—note how many traditional methods of spirituality include controlled breathing. One manager spent ten minutes before work meditating on the pile of papers on his desk—it could just as easily be machine parts in a factory, stock in a shop or the day's cooking. Others included reading which makes one take a fresh look at things, perhaps followed by quiet meditation or writing one's own responses. Art and music, religious or secular, will have an important place for some. A folder or scrap book of pictures, poems and experiences that have made a particular impression on us can be helpful. We waste many of our resources because we fail to put them where we can use them again.

I believe it is important that our disciplines should balance ways of looking inside ourselves with looking into the world and people around us. Spirituality is about a God who links the two. No doubt introverted and extroverted people will find themselves working with a different balance between these two. Our own internal preferences and fears have an important influence on the kinds of things we take seriously and what we prefer to ignore. Our unconscious fears are likely to be projected on to other people or groups who will then be rejected or dismissed. Recognising our own projections can be a constructive way to start facing ourselves. I have also found dream interpretation fruitful. The honest observations of husbands, wives and close friends can be helpful.

What is going on inside us has a strong and unseen influence on our reactions to the world and other people.

On the other hand, it is important in spirituality not to neglect what is going on in the world around us, particularly the ways in which we ourselves experience people and organizations. The kind of people we are is, in part, formed by or in reaction to the pressures of such forces on ourselves. We are created by our genetic inheritance, by the contexts and influences in which we live, grow up and work, and by our responses to these. What are the assumptions, values and dynamics that operate within these structures of life and how should we respond to them? Organisations have 'personalities', values, preferences and shadow sides, just as much as individuals.

Look at the assumptions pressed on people today by politics, companies and the media. Individualism suggests that we should all be self-sufficient. Money is seen as the only measure of value. Fun is assumed to be the main reason for doing things. Competition is the method for doing things. The time-scale is short-term. If those are really the assumptions that matter, we should not be surprised if selfishness and crime seem more prominent than they used to be. They need balancing by other attitudes that come from the love of God. Concern for the individual requires a strong sense that people belong together, must care for each other and have a sense of corporate welfare. Money is only a tool, not the main measure of value; people are the measure of value, if love matters. A sense of fun needs balancing by a strong sense of the constructive value of hard work, and perhaps even of suffering when the person concerned can accept it as creative. Competition needs balancing with a desire for co-operation. The time-scale that matters most, from a Christian point of view, is long-term, seeking lasting value and benefits. This is important to spirituality, because the kind of people we are is strongly influenced by the attitudes and assumptions of society, organizations and fashions around us. We accept them or react against them. Our view of life and humanity is strongly coloured by assumptions associated with science and technology, by current economic theory, by postmodern culture and the like. It is important to check how consistent these are with faith in a loving creator, revealed in Jesus of Nazareth and the theological models that flow from him. It is too easy to accept the bad and destructive features of our culture, along with its many good, constructive and caring aspects.

Spirituality in a Secular Age

It may seem to some that, because our churches tend to have modest congregations, there is little interest in the spiritual aspects of people and society. Others of us who meet many people with little or no involvement in regular church activities may have a different impression. Science, technology and economics continue to be very important, but the confidence that they will eventually answer all humanity's problems is dissipating. Many people are once again beginning to ask about the human aspects of our lives. Most of them seem to have little confidence in the Church's ability to help them in this. They do not understand the Church's language or ritual. Often they feel that the churches are out of touch with the lives of ordinary people. Frequently they themselves are out of date in their understanding of Church practice and theology. Yet many want to talk about spiritual things, not in ecclesiastical language, but in terms of the experiences and organizations, the views and questions which arise from their own lives.

In *The Language of Mystery*, Edward Robinson comments:

> If the traditional language of spirituality is, if no longer taboo, then at least for growing numbers of people no longer a credible option, the opportunities are infinitely expanded. If the energies of our spirituality are no longer confined to conventionally religious channels there is no limit to where they may appear. They are likely to leak out all over the place.[2]

Interest in spirituality does seem to be growing today, or perhaps is reawakening. It is rarely expressed in the language of the conventional Church. Often people do not identify it with things they assume the churches to be concerned about. Instead their interest in spirituality is seen in a variety of interests from business ethics to an increasingly widespread concern to keep fit; from a new interest in reincarnation, eastern meditation and New Age activities to a less focused interest in religious and human issues explored outside church organizations. The frequency of this less focused approach makes it difficult to see and encourage.

The churches need to grasp much more clearly the task of listening to people and organizations outside their boundaries, to discover their spiritual agenda and questionings, and to enter into a dialogue with them. In this dialogue, we and they can seek to learn from each other, and to

---

2. E. Robinson, *The Language of Mystery* (London: SCM Press, 1987), p. 90.

contribute our own experiences and understandings. Spirituality, in the future, is likely to look far less neat and tidy than in the past. Given the variety of people and their contexts, that is an asset.

INDEX OF NAMES